35 Hyggeli

RECIPES

To Get You Through
The Festive Season

Emma Alice Nilsson

Table of Contents

Introduction

Hygge, a Danish term that roughly translates to "coziness" or "comfort," holds a profound connection to the essence of Christmas. Rooted in creating warmth and togetherness, Hygge encompasses the spirit of the holiday season.

Put simply, it's about savoring intimate moments with loved ones, indulging in hot beverages by the fireplace, and adorning your home with soft, twinkling lights. During Christmas, the concept of Hygge truly shines as families gather around a beautifully decorated tree, exchange sincere gifts, and share filling meals.

The luminous glow of candles and the scent of freshly baked treats add to the Hygge tone, making it a time when everyone can loosen up, relax, and appreciate life's simple delights together. Ultimately, Hygge and Christmas are kindred spirits, both celebrating the warmth of human connections and the calmness of the season. Here, you can find 35 Hyggelig recipes to get you the festive season.

Embracing Coziness During the Festive Season

In the middle of a snow-covered world, we plunge headfirst into the magical joys of the festive season, all thanks to the Danish idea of Hygge. With warm shining lights, we wrap ourselves in comfy blankets, taking in the sweet smell of gingerbread cookies baking in the oven.

With flickering candles casting a warm and inviting light, we gather by the crackling fireplace, swapping stories and laughter while enveloped in the comforting embrace of oversized sweaters.

This cherished tradition beckons us to revel in life's simple joys—a mug of aromatic mulled wine cradled in our hands—as we immerse ourselves in the elusive spirit of Hygge, akin to unwrapping a mystery hidden deep within the heart of the season itself.

Chapter 1: Hygge Appetizers

Christmas Charcuterie Board

Embrace the warmth and coziness of the holiday season with this delightful Christmas Charcuterie Board. Whether hosting a festive gathering or simply looking to elevate your snack game, this spread is a perfect way to infuse a touch of Hygge into your Christmas celebrations.

In a delightful union of flavors, this charcuterie board effortlessly marries the savory and sweet, fusing a plethora of tastes, textures, and hues that promise to captivate your guests. Seize the moment, call everyone to the fireside, ignite a cluster of candles, and let the

Hygge ambiance gently embrace your surroundings while you relish this alluring, visually striking Christmas delicacy.

Yield: +- 6-8 Servings

Ingredients you will need for this recipe:

- 150g (5.3 oz.) Prosciutto
- 150g (5.3 oz.) Salami
- 150g (5.3 oz.) Chorizo
- 150g (5.3 oz.) Smoked Gouda cheese
- 150g (5.3 oz.) Brie cheese
- 150g (5.3 oz.) Manchego cheese
- ½ Cup (125g/4.4 oz.) mixed olives
- ½ Cup (125g/4.4 oz.) roasted almonds
- ½ Cup (125g4.4 oz.) dried cranberries
- ½ Cup (125g/4.4 oz.) fresh grapes
- ¼ Cup (60g/2.1 oz.) whole grain mustard
- ¼ Cup (60g/2.1 oz.) honey

Items needed for the garnishes:

- Fresh rosemary sprigs
- Edible flowers (optional)
- Crackers and bread slices

Instructions:

1. Arrange a large wooden or slate board on your table, creating a visually appealing base for your Christmas Charcuterie Board.
2. Start building your charcuterie selection by artfully folding or rolling the prosciutto, Salami, and chorizo onto different board sections. Allow them to overlap slightly for an inviting display.
3. Cut the Smoked Gouda, Brie, and Manchego cheeses into bite-sized pieces and arrange them alongside the cured meats.
4. Scatter mixed olives, roasted almonds, and dried cranberries, filling in the gaps between the meats and cheeses.

5. Add fresh grapes for a natural sweetness, placing them in clusters for an appealing arrangement.
6. In a small bowl, combine the whole-grain mustard and honey. Place it in the board's center, giving your guests a tangy and sweet dipping sauce.
7. For a festive touch, tuck fresh rosemary sprigs between the ingredients, adding flavor and a delightful aroma.
8. Elevate the visual appeal with a subtle sprinkle of edible blooms, should you desire to add an extra touch of charm to the presentation.
9. Serve your Christmas Charcuterie Board with an assortment of crackers and bread slices to create the perfect bite-sized combinations.

Nutritional Info (Per Serving):

Calories: 380
Protein: 18g
Carbohydrates: 28g
Fat: 24g

Creamy Butternut Squash Soup with Crispy Bacon

Indulge in the warm embrace of Hygge this Christmas season with a soul-soothing bowl of Creamy Butternut Squash Soup with Crispy Bacon. This delightful recipe effortlessly combines the earthy sweetness of roasted butternut squash with the savory crunch of crispy bacon.

It's the perfect comfort food to warm your heart and create cozy moments during the festive holidays. It perfectly symbolizes the Danish concept of Hygge, bringing warmth and comfort to all your festive gatherings.

Yield: +- 6 Servings

Ingredients you will need for this recipe:

For the Soup:

- 1 Large butternut squash (approximately 2 pounds or 900 grams), peeled, seeded, and cubed
- 2 Tablespoons of olive oil (30ml)(1.01 fl oz.)
- 1 Medium onion, chopped
- 3 Finely cut garlic cloves,
- 4 Cups of store bought or homemade vegetable broth (1000ml)(33.8 fl oz.)
- Dried thyme, 1 teaspoon (4g)(0.14 oz.)
- Half a teaspoon of ground nutmeg (2 g)(0.07 oz)
- Salt & pepper, (For own taste preference)
- 1 Cup Heavy cream, (250ml) (8.5 fl oz.)

Bacon:

- 6 slices of streaky bacon (Or bacon of your choice)
- 1 tablespoon maple syrup (15ml)(0.5 fl oz.)

Instructions:

1. Preheat your gas or convection oven to 400°F (200°C).
2. Place the cubed butternut squash on a baking sheet and drizzle with olive oil. Season with your desired amount of salt and pepper. Roast in the oven for 30-35 minutes or until the squash is tender and slightly caramelized.
3. Heat about one tablespoon of olive oil in a large soup pot over a moderate heat. Next, incorporate the minced garlic and diced onion. Sauté until the onions turn translucent, about 5 minutes.
4. Add the roasted butternut squash into the soup pot, followed by the vegetable broth(either store bought or homemade), ground nutmeg, salt, pepper, and dried thyme. Bring the roasted butternut squash soup to a simmer, cover, and cook for 15-20 minutes, allowing the flavors to meld together.
5. Use a stick or immersion blender to blend the roasted butternut squash soup until creamy and lump-free. Alternatively, you can transfer the roasted butternut squash

soup in batches to your blender, but be cautious when blending hot liquids.

6. Return the blended roasted butternut squash soup to the pot, stirring in the fresh heavy cream. Simmer for an additional 5 minutes, allowing the cream to incorporate fully. Alter the seasoning to suit your taste.

7. Prepare the crispy bacon While the roasted butternut squash soup is simmering. Over medium-high heat, cook the streaky bacon (or bacon of your choice) in a separate skillet until it becomes crispy. Drizzle maple syrup over the bacon during the last few minutes of cooking, allowing it to caramelize slightly. Once done, remove the bacon from the skillet and place it on paper towels to drain excess grease.

8. Serve the Creamy Butternut Squash Soup hot, garnished with crumbled crispy bacon. Allow the warmth and richness of this soup to envelop you in a cozy hygge experience.

Nutritional Info (Per Serving):

Calories: 350
Protein: 5g
Carbohydrates: 29g
Fat: 24g

Danish Smørrebrød: Open-Faced Sandwiches

Embrace the cozy spirit of Hygge this Christmas season with a delightful Danish classic - Smørrebrød! These open-faced sandwiches perfectly embody comfort, simplicity, and elegance, making them an ideal addition to your festive table. Expertly curated from a thoughtful selection of ingredients, these Smørrebrød present an intricate tapestry of tastes and sensations that embrace your senses and gratify your taste buds.

Whether relished as an appetizer, a quick bite, or a modest repast, these Nordic delights undeniably infuse an enchanting touch of Danish allure into your seasonal get-togethers. Indulge in the inviting embrace of Danish Smørrebrød as you gather with loved ones during the festive season.

These open-faced sandwiches seamlessly infuse your Christmas celebrations with the cozy essence of Hygge, allowing everyone to relish the delightful combination of camaraderie and exceptional cuisine.

Yield: 4 Smørrebrød

Ingredients you will need for this recipe:

- 4 Slices of dense rye bread
- 4 oz. (115g) Of smoked salmon
- 4 oz. (115g) Of roast beef, thinly sliced
- 4 oz. (115g) Of pickled herring
- 4 Hard-boiled eggs, sliced
- 4 Tablespoons of remoulade sauce (59.14ml)(2 fl oz.)
- 4 Tablespoons of creamy horseradish sauce (59.14ml)(2 fl oz.)
- 4 Radishes, thinly sliced
- 1 Small red onion, thinly sliced
- 2 Tablespoons of capers (29.57ml)(1 fl oz.)
- Fresh dill sprigs for garnish
- Salt and pepper, to taste

Instructions:

1. Start by preparing your dense rye bread slices. They should be firm enough to support the toppings without becoming soggy. Trim the crusts if desired.
2. Lay out the rye bread slices on a clean surface.
3. For each open-faced sandwich, begin with a base layer of remoulade sauce, generously spread over the bread.
4. Arrange the ingredients creatively on top of the remoulade sauce for each sandwich:
   A. For the smoked salmon Smørrebrød:
   B. Artfully lay out the smoked salmon slices in a mysteriously beguiling mosaic of dispersion.
5. Garnish generously with zesty capers, lively dill, and red onion rings in elegant circles.
6. For the roast beef Smørrebrød:
   A. Gently place the roast beef slices on the surface.

    B. Now, add a sprinkle of radish slices, and just a dash of freshly ground pepper.
7. For the pickled herring Smørrebrød:
    A. Assemble, one by one, those tangy pickled herring filets.
    B. Place upon them, in deliberate fashion, the resilient discs of hard-boiled eggs and the minuscule fragments of crimson onion.
8. For the egg and horseradish Smørrebrød:
    A. Smear a generous layer of velvety horseradish sauce, creating a canvas.
    B. With utmost precision, delicately lay out the hard-boiled egg slices, expertly weaving them together.
9. Finish each Smørrebrød with a final garnish of fresh dill.
10. Season each sandwich with a dash of salt and freshly ground pepper, as per your preference.
11. Serve your Danish Smørrebrød on a platter, and let your guests enjoy these open-faced sandwiches' delightful flavors and textures.

Nutritional Info (Per Serving):

Calories: 300
Protein: 20g
Carbohydrates: 22g
Fat: 15g

Cranberry and Brie Puff Pastry Bites

Indulge in the warm embrace of the holiday season with these Cranberry and Brie Puff Pastry Bites. A delightful blend of flaky puff pastry, creamy brie cheese, and tart cranberry sauce, these delectable bites encapsulate the essence of Hygge, making your Christmas celebrations cozy and heartwarming. Ideal for sharing with loved ones or savoring as a personal treat, these appetizers are a true embodiment of comfort and joy.

Yield: +- 12 Cranberry and Brie Puff Pastry Bites

Ingredients you will need for this recipe:

- 1 Sheet of puff pastry, thawed (approximately 23 x 23 centimeters or 9 x 9 inches)

- ½ A cup (125g)(4.4 oz.) of brie cheese, cut into small cubes
- ¼ A cup (59.14ml)(2 fl oz.) of cranberry sauce
- 1 Egg, beaten (for egg wash)
- Fresh rosemary sprigs for garnish (optional)
- Salt and pepper to your desired taste

Instructions:

1. Preheat your convection or gas oven to 375°F (190°C) while you line a baking sheet with parchment paper.
2. Next, roll out the thawed puff pastry sheet on a lightly floured surface. Cut it into small squares, roughly 2x2 inches (5x5 cm).
3. Place a cube of brie cheese in the center of each pastry square. Top it with a small dollop of cranberry sauce, seasoning with a pinch of salt, and a dash of black pepper.
4. Carefully fold the pastry squares over the filling to create triangular-shaped parcels. Press the puff pastry edges with a fork to seal them, ensuring no filling escapes during baking.
5. Arrange the filled pastry bites on the pre-lined baking sheet, leaving some space between each one.
6. Brush the tops of the pastry bites with the beaten egg, giving them a beautiful golden finish when baked.
7. Garnish each bite with a small rosemary sprig for an extra touch of holiday elegance.
8. Bake in the oven for approximately 15-18 minutes or until the Brie puff pastry bites turn golden brown and puff beautifully.
9. Remove from the oven, allowing the Cranberry and Brie Puff Pastry Bites to cool slightly before serving.
10. Serve these delightful bites warm and watch as they disappear quickly. They make for a wonderful appetizer during your Christmas gatherings or as a cozy snack by the fireside.

Nutritional Info (Per Serving):

Calories: 168
Protein: 4g

Carbohydrates: 11g
Fat: 12g

Roasted Chestnuts with Sea Salt

Indulge in the ultimate Christmas comfort food with these Roasted Chestnuts with a hint of Sea Salt. The crackling warmth of an open fire, the cozy embrace of soft blankets, and the earthy aroma of roasted chestnuts – all the elements of Hygge come together in this simple yet delightful recipe.

Perfect for sharing with family and friends as you create cherished holiday memories together. Enjoy the simple pleasures of Hygge this Christmas with these delectable Roasted Chestnuts with Sea Salt.

Yield: 4 Servings

Ingredients you will need for this recipe:

- 1 Pound (450g)(15.87 oz.) of fresh chestnuts
- 1 Teaspoon sea salt (4 g)(0.14 oz)

Instructions:

1. First things first, begin by preheating your gas or convection oven to roughly 425°F (220°C).
2. Using a sharp knife, make a small cross-shaped incision on the flat side of each chestnut. This allows steam to escape during roasting and prevents them from exploding.
3. Place the prepared chestnuts on a lined baking sheet, ensuring they are in a single even layer. This ensures even roasting. Pop them into the preheated oven.
4. Roast the chestnuts for about 20-25 minutes, or until the shells have split open, revealing the tender, fragrant chestnut inside. Give them a shake or stir occasionally to ensure they roast evenly.
5. Remove the chestnuts from the oven, allowing them to cool slightly until you can handle them comfortably. Then, while they're still warm, peel off the tough outer shell and the thin inner skin. This is easier to do while they're warm.
6. Once peeled, transfer the chestnuts to a bowl and sprinkle them with a teaspoon of sea salt. Toss them gently to coat the warm chestnuts with the salt evenly.
7. These Roasted Chestnuts with Sea Salt are best enjoyed warm. Serve them in a festive bowl or rustic platter for a touch of hygge charm.

Nutritional Info (Per Serving):

Calories: 180
Protein: 2g
Carbohydrates: 41g
Fat: 1g

Chapter 2: Comforting Hygge Mains

Classic Roast Turkey With Sage & Cranberry Sauce

Indulge in the heartwarming embrace of Hygge this Christmas season with our Classic Roast Turkey, lovingly prepared to perfection and served with a delightful Sage and Cranberry Sauce. This timeless recipe embodies the essence of comfort and togetherness, making it an ideal centerpiece for your festive gathering.

Yield: +-8 Servings

Ingredients:

- 1 Whole turkey (12-14 Lbs or 5.4-6.4 kg)
- ½ A cup (125ml/4.2 fl oz.) unsalted butter, softened
- 2 Tablespoons (30g/1.05 oz.) of fresh sage leaves, finely chopped
- Salt and pepper to your desired taste
- 2 Cups (500ml/16.9 fl oz.) chicken or turkey broth
- 1 Cup (250g/8.8 oz.) fresh cranberries
- ½ A cup (125ml/4.2 fl oz.) of orange juice
- ¼ A cup (60ml/2.02 fl oz.) maple syrup
- ¼ A cup (60ml/2.02 fl oz.) red wine
- ¼ A cup (60ml/2.02 fl oz.) water
- 2 Tablespoons (30g/1.05 oz.) of plain flour

Instructions:

1. Preheat your oven to around 325°F (160°C). Thoroughly rinse the turkey inside and out, then pat it dry with paper towels. Place the turkey in a roasting pan with a roasting rack.
2. Combine the softened butter, chopped sage, salt, and pepper in a small bowl. Gently loosen the turkey's skin, taking care not to tear it, and spread the sage butter mixture evenly under the skin. Season the outside of the turkey with additional salt and pepper.
3. Pour 1 cup (250g/8.8 oz.) of turkey or chicken broth into the base of the roasting pan. Cover the turkey loosely with aluminum foil. Place the turkey in the oven and roast for about 3 to 3.5 hours, or until the internal temperature of the turkey's thigh reaches 165°F (74°C). Baste the turkey every 30 minutes with pan juices for that perfect golden skin.
4. You can prepare the cranberry sauce while the turkey is roasting. Combine the fresh cranberries, orange juice, maple syrup, red wine, and water in a saucepan. Bring the cranberry, orange juice, maple syrup, red wine, and water mixture to a simmer over medium heat, stirring occasionally.

Cook for about 15 minutes or until the cranberries burst and the sauce thickens slightly.

5. Mix two tablespoons of plain flour in a small mixing bowl with the leftover cup of chicken or turkey broth. Stir until smooth. Gradually add this mixture to the cranberry sauce, stirring continuously. Simmer for an additional 5 minutes until the sauce reaches your desired consistency—season with salt and pepper to your desired taste.

6. Once the turkey is fully cooked, remove it from the oven and let it rest for about 20-30 minutes before carving.

7. Serve the Classic Roast Turkey with slices of succulent meat drizzled with the Sage and Cranberry Sauce. Garnish with extra sage leaves for a festive touch.

Nutritional Info (Per Serving):

Calories: 350
Protein: 7g
Carbohydrates: 19g
Fat: 31g

Slow-Cooked Beef Stew with Root Vegetables

A slow-cooked beef stew with root vegetables is a delicious and comforting meal. The slow cooking process tenderizes the beef and allows the flavors of the vegetables to merge. The most common root vegetables in stews are potatoes, carrots, and parsnips. For added flavor, add any other vegetables you like, like onions and celery.

Yield: +- 6 Servings

Ingredients:

- 2 Pounds (900g) beef stew meat, cut into bite-sized pieces
- 2 Tablespoons (30ml/1.05 oz.) vegetable oil
- 1 Large onion, chopped

- 3 Minced cloves of garlic
- 3 Carrots, peeled and sliced into rounds (roughly 1 cup or 250g/8.8 oz.)
- 3 Parsnips, peeled and chopped into chunks (about 1 cup or 250g/8.8 oz.)
- 2 Celery stalks, chopped (about ½ a cup or 125g/4.4 oz.)
- 3 Potatoes, peeled and diced (about 1 ½ cups or 375g/13.2 oz.)
- 1 Cup (250g/8.8 oz.) green beans, trimmed and cut into 1-inch pieces
- 1 Can (14 oz./400g) diced tomatoes
- 4 Cups (1000ml/33.8 fl oz.) beef broth
- 2 Bay leaves
- 1 Teaspoon (5g/0.17 oz.) dried thyme
- 1 Teaspoon (5g0/17 oz.) dried rosemary
- Salt and pepper to your desired taste
- 2 Tablespoons (30g/1.05 oz.) plain flour
- 2 Tablespoons (30ml/1.01 fl oz.) water
- Chopped fresh parsley for garnish (optional)

Instructions:

1. Heat the vegetable oil over medium-high heat in a large skillet or frying pan. Add the beef stewing meat and brown on all sides. Transfer the browned stewing meat to a plate and set aside.
2. Next, add the finely chopped onion and minced garlic in the same skillet. Sauté for 2-3 minutes until fragrant and the onions become translucent.
3. Mix the flour and water in a small bowl to make a smooth paste. This will help thicken the stew later.
4. In a large slow cooker, combine the browned beef, sautéed onions and garlic, chopped carrots, parsnips, celery, diced potatoes, green beans, and diced tomatoes.
5. Next, pour the beef broth over the ingredients in the slow cooker. Add the bay leaves, dried thyme, dried rosemary, salt, and pepper. Stir everything well to combine.

6. Cover the slow cooker, allowing it to cook on the low setting for 8 hours or until the beef is tender and the vegetables are cooked through.
7. About 30 minutes before serving, remove the bay leaves from the stew. Then, slowly pour in the flour-water mixture while stirring continuously to thicken the stew. Let it cook for an additional 30 minutes.
8. Taste the stew and adjust the seasoning with salt and pepper if needed.
9. Serve the hearty slow-cooked beef stew with root vegetables in bowls, garnished with chopped fresh parsley if desired.

Nutritional Info (Per Serving):

Calories: 350
Protein: 26g
Carbohydrates: 40g
Fat: 10g

Vegetarian Mushroom Wellington

Incorporating a symphony of herbs, mushrooms, and cheese, the Vegetarian Mushroom Wellington emerges as the quintessential plant-based creation, its essence woven delicately into the layers of a flaky puff pastry. A gastronomic delight for the plant-loving palate, this offering is a testament to a meatless main course's flavorful and fulfilling possibilities.

Yield: 6 Servings

Ingredients:

- Two sheets of puff pastry (each 320g / 11.3 oz.)
- (500g / 17.6 oz.) of fresh mushrooms, finely chopped
- (200g / 7 oz.) of fresh spinach, chopped

- One small onion, finely diced
- Three minced cloves of garlic
- Two tablespoons (29.6ml/1 fl oz.) of olive oil
- One teaspoon (15g/0.5 oz.) of fresh thyme leaves
- One teaspoon (15g/0.5 oz.) of fresh rosemary, finely chopped
- ½ A cup (125g/4.4 oz.) of breadcrumbs
- ½ A cup (125g/4.4 oz.) of grated Parmesan cheese
- Salt and black pepper, to taste
- One egg, beaten (for egg wash)

Instructions:

1. Preheat oven to 392°F (200°C)
2. Heat a small amount of olive oil over moderate heat in a large skillet. Add diced garlic and onion, sautéing until they turn translucent for about 3-4 minutes.
3. Next, add the finely chopped mushrooms into the skillet and cook until all their moisture has evaporated, stirring occasionally. This should take about 10-12 minutes.
4. Stir in the chopped spinach, thyme, rosemary, breadcrumbs, and Parmesan cheese. Cook for an additional 2-3 minutes, until the spinach is wilted and the mixture is well combined—season with salt and black pepper to your desired taste.
5. Following this, roll out a sheet of puff pastry and place it on a flat baking pan lined with baking paper.
6. Spoon the mushroom and spinach filling onto the center of the puff pastry, leaving some space around the edges.
7. Next, roll out the other sheet of puff pastry and place it over the filling. Press the two pastry sheets' edges together to seal the Wellington.
8. Use a sharp knife to make decorative cuts or patterns on the top of the Wellington, then brush the surface with the beaten egg for a golden finish.
9. Oven bake the pastry for 30-35 min, or until crisp and golden brown.

Nutritional Info (Per Serving):

Calories: 350 kcal
Protein: 10g
Carbohydrates: 31g
Fat: 21g

Norwegian Salmon With Dill and Mustard Sauce

Originating in Norway, the well-loved Norwegian Salmon with Dill and Mustard Sauce is a staple that marries grilled or pan-fried salmon filets with a zesty, aromatic concoction, blending dill, mustard, and cream.

This symphony of flavors, uniting the luscious, oily salmon with the vibrant and zesty notes of dill and mustard, creates a profoundly gratifying and delectable feast. Alongside this splendid dish, your side options are wide open – think steamed asparagus, irresistible roasted potatoes, or even a straightforward green salad. Mix and match to craft your perfect, satisfying meal.

Yield: 4 Servings

Ingredients:

For Salmon:

- 4 Fresh Norwegian salmon filets (6 oz. / 170g each)
- 2 Tablespoons olive oil (30 ml/1.01 fl oz.)
- Salt and pepper, to taste
- 1 Lemon, sliced for garnish

For the Dill and Mustard Sauce:

- ½ A cup mayonnaise (125ml/4.2 fl oz.)
- 2 Tablespoons Dijon mustard (30ml/1.01 oz.)
- 1 Tablespoon honey (15ml/0.5 fl oz.)
- 2 Tablespoons of fresh dill, finely chopped (30g/1.05 oz.)
- 1 Tablespoon of fresh lemon juice (15ml/0.5 oz.)
- 1 Clove garlic, minced
- Salt and pepper, to taste

Instructions:

1. Preheat your oven to roughly 375°F (190°C).
2. Prepare the Salmon:
   A. Arrange your recently procured salmon filets meticulously upon a baking sheet thoughtfully lined with parchment paper.
   B. Spoon some olive oil onto those salmon filets, then give them a sprinkle of salt and pepper.
   C. Position several lemon slices atop each filet in no particular order.
3. Next, bake the salmon in the preheated oven for about 12-15 minutes or until the salmon flakes easily with a fork. The salmon's cooking time might vary slightly based on the thickness of your filets.

4. While the salmon is baking in the oven, prepare the dill and mustard sauce:
   A. Whisk together mayonnaise, Dijon mustard, honey, fresh dill, lemon juice, salt, minced garlic, and pepper in a small bowl. Adjust the seasoning to your taste.
5. Once the salmon is done baking, remove it from the oven and let it rest for a minute or two.
6. Serve the salmon filets on individual plates and drizzle the dill and mustard sauce generously over each filet.
7. Garnish with extra fresh dill and lemon slices, if desired.
8. Enjoy your delicious Norwegian Salmon with Dill and Mustard Sauce!

Nutritional Info (Per Serving):

Calories: 350
Protein: 30g
Carbohydrates: 8g
Fat: 22g

Stuffed Bell Peppers with Wild Rice and Cranberries

The tantalizing union of wild rice and cranberries nestled within stuffed bell peppers isn't just your everyday meal. No, siree! It's a veritable nutritional powerhouse, a medley of flavors and benefits that'll have you scratching your head in amazement. Wild rice? Absolutely! It's bringing the fiber and protein game to the table.

Cranberries, on the other hand, pack a punch with their antioxidant-rich goodness. Moreover, let's not forget those bell peppers, champions of vitamin C and cholesterol's sworn enemies. Prepare to be baffled by the sheer perfection of this dish; it's not just healthy – it's mind-bogglingly satisfying!

Yield: 4 Servings

Ingredients:

For the Stuffed Bell Peppers:

- 4 Large bell peppers (any color)
- 1 Cup (250g/8.8 oz.) wild rice
- 2 Cups (500ml/16.9 fl oz.) vegetable broth
- 1 Cup (250ml/8.8 fl oz.) water
- 1 Small onion, finely chopped
- 2 Minced cloves of garlic
- 1 Cup (250g/8.8 oz.) dried cranberries
- 1 Cup (250g/8.8 oz.) chopped mushrooms
- 1 Cup (250g/8.8 oz.) diced tomatoes
- 1 Cup (250g/8.8 oz.) cooked chickpeas (canned or pre-cooked)
- 1 Teaspoon (15ml/0.5 fl oz.) olive oil
- 1 Teaspoon (15g/0.53 oz.) of dried thyme
- Salt and pepper to your desired taste

For the Tomato Sauce:

- 1 Can (400g/14.10 oz.) crushed tomatoes
- ½ (0.08 oz.) a teaspoon dried basil
- ½ (0.08 oz.) a teaspoon dried oregano
- Salt and pepper to your desired taste

Instructions:

1. Preheat your oven to around 375°F (190°C).
2. Rinse the wild rice thoroughly in cold water. Combine the wild rice, vegetable broth, and water in a medium saucepan. Bring the wild rice, vegetable broth, and water mix to a rolling boil, reduce the heat to low, cover, and simmer for about 45-50 minutes or until the rice is soft and almost all the liquid is absorbed. Remove from heat and let it cool.
3. While the rice is cooking, cut the tops off the bell peppers, removing any seeds and membranes. Set them aside.

4. Heat the olive oil over moderate heat in a large skillet. Add the chopped onions and garlic. Sauté for 2-3 minutes until they become translucent.
5. Add the chopped mushrooms, diced tomatoes, and cooked chickpeas to the skillet. Cook for another 5 minutes, stirring occasionally.
6. Combine the cooked wild rice, cranberries, and sautéed mushroom mixture in a large mixing bowl—season with dried thyme, salt, and pepper. Mix everything thoroughly.
7. Stuff the cut bell peppers with the rice and mushroom mixture, pressing down gently to pack the filling.
8. Place the stuffed peppers in a baking dish.
9. Mix the crushed tomatoes with dried basil, dried oregano, pepper, and salt in a separate bowl. Pour this tomato sauce over the stuffed peppers.
10. Cover the baking dish filled with stuffed peppers with aluminum foil and oven-bake for 35-40 minutes or until the peppers are tender.
11. Remove from the oven, uncover, and bake for an additional 10 minutes to allow the tops to brown slightly.

Nutritional Info (Per Serving):

Calories: 330
Protein: 8g
Carbohydrates: 73g
Fat: 2g

Chapter 3:Cozy Sides and Salads

Creamy Mashed Potatoes with Garlic and Chives

Indulge in the warm embrace of the holiday season with our delightful recipe for Creamy Mashed Potatoes with Garlic and Chives. This comforting side dish encapsulates the essence of Hygge, bringing simplicity and coziness to your Christmas table.

These mashed potatoes, velvety and rich, are a perfect addition to your festive spread. The gentle infusion of garlic adds a subtle depth of flavor, while the chives contribute a mild, fresh zing. Together, they harmonize in a symphony of taste that will leave your loved ones longing for more.

In the spirit of the season, we present you with a nourishing and soothing recipe, creating a sense of togetherness at the heart of the Hygge philosophy. Share the warmth, gather around the table, and savor every bite of these Creamy Mashed Potatoes with Garlic and Chives this Christmas.

Yield: 6 Servings

Ingredients:

- 2 pounds (907.2g) russet potatoes, peeled and cut into 1-inch chunks
- Four cloves of garlic, minced
- ½ a cup (125ml/ 4.2 fl oz.) whole milk
- ½ a cup (125g/ 4.4 oz.) unsalted butter
- Salt and black pepper, to taste
- Two tablespoons (30g/1.06 oz.) of fresh chives, finely chopped

Instructions:

1. Start by placing the peeled and diced potatoes in a medium to large pot. Add cold water to cover them and season generously with salt. Bring the liquid to a boil over an intense heat and then lower the heat to a simmer. Cook the potatoes for 15-20 minutes or until juicy enough to be easily pierced with a fork.
2. While the potatoes are simmering, in a separate saucepan, melt the butter over low heat. Add the minced garlic, allowing it to infuse into the butter. Cook gently for 1-2 minutes, but do not let the garlic brown.
3. When the potatoes are juicy, drain them thoroughly. Please return them to the pot and let them sit for a minute to allow excess moisture to evaporate.

4. Mash the potatoes, utilizing a potato masher or a ricer for a smoother texture. Incorporate the garlic-infused butter, followed by the whole milk. Continue mashing until the potatoes are silky and creamy. Season amply with salt and freshly ground black pepper.
5. Sprinkle the chopped chives over the creamy mashed potatoes and gently fold them, reserving a few for garnish.
6. Move the mashed potatoes to a serving dish and garnish with the remaining chives. Serve immediately, and watch your guests savor the heartwarming goodness.

Nutritional Info (Per Serving):

Calories: 330
Protein: 4g
Carbohydrates: 35g
Fat: 19g

Brussels Sprouts with Maple Glaze and Pecans

Those wholesome little gems of Brussels sprouts make a splendid and delectable complement to any dining occasion. It is packed with plenty of fibers and a whole lot of antioxidants. A drizzle of maple glaze presents a delightful sweetness, creating a sticky coating, while the pecans offer a satisfying crunch. Whether you seek a healthful and flavorsome side dish or a delectable topping for your meat or fish, this dish will warm your heart during the festive season.

Yield: 4 Servings

Ingredients:

- 500g (1 lb/17.63 oz) fresh Brussels sprouts, trimmed and halved
- 158g (2/3 cup/5.6 oz.) pecan halves
- Three tablespoons (44.4ml)(1.05 fl oz.) pure maple syrup
- Two tablespoons (29.6ml)(1 fl oz.) olive oil
- One teaspoon (5ml)(0.2 fl oz.) balsamic vinegar
- ½ a teaspoon (2.8g)(0.1 oz) sea salt
- ¼ teaspoon (1.42g)(0.05 oz) freshly ground black pepper
- ¼ teaspoon (1.42g)(0.05 oz) ground cinnamon

Instructions:

1. Warm up your oven to 200°C (400°F).
2. In a large mixing bowl, combine the trimmed and halved Brussels sprouts with the olive oil, sea salt, and freshly ground black pepper. Toss to coat them evenly.
3. Unroll the Brussels sprouts on a baking sheet in a single layer. Roast them in the oven for about 20-25 minutes or until tender and slightly caramelized. Give them a gentle stir halfway through the roasting time for even browning.
4. While the Brussels sprouts are roasting, let's prepare the maple glaze. Heat the maple syrup, balsamic vinegar, and ground cinnamon over medium-low heat in a small saucepan. Stir gently until the blend thickens slightly, about 3-4 minutes. Remove it from the heat.
5. In a separate dry skillet, toast the pecan halves over medium heat for 2-3 minutes until they become fragrant and slightly browned. Be cautious not to burn them.
6. Once the Brussels sprouts are done roasting, transport them to a serving platter.
7. Drizzle the maple glaze over the roasted Brussels sprouts and toss gently to coat.
8. Sprinkle the toasted pecans for that perfect balance of textures and flavors.
9. Serve immediately, and savor the delicious harmony of comfort and festivity.

Nutritional Info (Per Serving):

Calories: 220
Protein: 4g
Carbohydrates: 21g
Fat: 15g

Scandinavian Red Cabbage Salad

In the heart of a cozy festive celebration, this Scandinavian Red Cabbage Salad brings a delightful touch of warmth to your table. Its vibrant hues and comforting flavors make it the perfect addition to your Hygge-inspired festivities.

This simple yet inviting dish combines crisp red cabbage, a hint of sweet apple, and a zesty dressing, creating a harmonious medley that will envelop your taste buds in a hug of seasonal comfort. So, gather your loved ones, set the table with this nourishing creation, and savor the joy of a Hygge-inspired Christmas meal.

Yield: 6 Servings

Ingredients:

- One small head of red cabbage (about 500g/17.64 oz.)
- Two apples (choose your favorite variety)
- One small red onion
- ¼ cup (60ml/2.03 fl oz.) apple cider vinegar
- ¼ cup (60ml2.03 fl oz.) olive oil
- Two tablespoons (30ml/1.01 fl oz.) honey
- 1 teaspoon (5g/0.18 oz.) ground cinnamon
- ½ a teaspoon (2.8g)(0.1 oz.) ground cloves
- Salt and ground black pepper to your desired taste
- Chopped fresh parsley for garnish

Instructions:

1. Start by finely shredding the red cabbage using a sharp knife or a mandoline. Place the minced cabbage in a large mixing bowl.
2. Peel and core the apples, then carve them into tiny, matchstick-like strips. Add them to the bowl with the cabbage.
3. Cut the red onion into thin rings and add them to the mixture of cabbage and apples.
4. Whip together the apple cider vinegar, olive oil, honey, ground cinnamon, cloves, salt, and black pepper in a separate bowl. This creates a flavorful dressing.
5. Pour the relish over the cabbage, apples, and onion. Toss everything gently to ensure that the dressing coats all the ingredients evenly.
6. Close the dish with plastic wrap or a lid and refrigerate for about 1 hour, allowing the flavors to meld and the salad to marinate.
7. Before serving, give the salad one last stir to ensure it's well-mixed. Taste and adjust the seasoning if necessary.

8. Sprinkle freshly chopped parsley over the top for freshness and color.

Nutritional Information (Per Serving):

Calories: 150
Protein: 1g
Carbohydrates: 21g
Fat: 7g

Warm Quinoa Salad with Fresh Roasted Vegetables

In the heart of the festive season, we yearn for comfort and warmth, a sense of Hygge that envelops us. Our Cozy Christmas Quinoa Salad with Fresh Roasted Veggies perfectly embodies this desire.

Delight in the simple yet delightful combination of quinoa and freshly roasted vegetables, crafted to soothe your soul and bring Christmas magic to your table. This recipe effortlessly encapsulates the essence of hygge, inviting you to savor every bite of the holiday season.

Yield: 4 Servings

Ingredients:

- (250g/8.8 oz.) or 1 cup of quinoa
- 2 cups (500ml/16.9 fl oz.) water
- 2 cups (500g/17.6 oz.) mixed vegetables (carrots, bell peppers, red onion, and zucchini)
- Two tablespoons (30ml/1.01 fl oz.) olive oil
- One teaspoon (5ml/0.16 oz) balsamic vinegar
- One teaspoon (5ml/0.17 fl oz.) honey
- One teaspoon (5ml/0.17 fl oz.) of Dijon mustard
- Salt and pepper, to taste
- Two tablespoons (10g/0.35 oz) fresh parsley, chopped
- ¼ cup (85g/3 oz.) of feta cheese, crumbled

Instructions:

1. Heat up your oven to 425°F (220°C).
2. Thoroughly wash the quinoa in a fine mesh strainer, then merge it with 2 cups of water in a medium saucepan. Bring the water to a boil over medium-high temperature, then lower the heat to low, cover, and let it boil gently for about 15 minutes, or till the quinoa is cooked and the water is absorbed. Take it off the heat and let it cool down for 5 minutes, then fluff it with a fork.
3. As the quinoa cooks, gather the roasted vegetables. Dice the mixed veg into small cubed-sized pieces, placing them on a flat baking pan. Drizzle the olive oil over the mixed vegetables, flavor with pepper and salt, and toss to coat.

Roast in the oven for 20-25 minutes or until the vegetables are tender and slightly caramelized.

4. Combine balsamic vinegar, honey, Dijon mustard, and a drizzle of salt and pepper to create the dressing in a small dish.
5. In a large serving dish, mix the cooked roasted vegetables and quinoa. Drizzle the balsamic dressing over the mixture and gently toss to coat all ingredients evenly.
6. Sprinkle the chopped fresh parsley and crumbled feta cheese over the top.

Nutritional Information (Per Serving):

Calories: 280
Protein: 7g
Carbohydrates: 38g
Fat: 11g

Danish Potato Salad with Pickles and Dill

Introducing our delightful Danish Potato Salad with Pickles and Dill. This comforting dish embodies the essence of Hygge, making it the perfect addition to your Christmas season festivities. With simple, rustic ingredients and a heartwarming flavor, it will give you a sense of coziness and togetherness.

In this recipe, we'll guide you through creating a nourishing side dish that's sure to add a smile to your face during the holiday season. Get ready to embrace the warmth of the Danish tradition and share the joy with your loved ones as you savor each bite of this classic potato salad.

Yield: 6 Servings

Ingredients:

- 2 pounds (907.2g/32 oz.) potatoes, preferably waxy, peeled and cut into bite-sized cubes
- ½ a cup (125ml/4.2 fl oz.) mayonnaise
- ¼ cup (60ml/2.03 fl oz.) sour cream
- Three tablespoons (44.4ml/1.50 fl oz.) white vinegar
- Two tablespoons (30ml/1.01 fl oz.) Dijon mustard
- One tablespoon (15ml/0.51 fl oz.) honey
- ½ a cup (125g/4.4 oz) dill pickles, finely chopped
- Two tablespoons (30g/1.06 oz) red onion, finely minced
- Two tablespoons (30g/1.06 oz) fresh dill, finely chopped
- Salt and black pepper, to taste

Instructions:

1. Place the potato cubes in a big pot of cold, salted water. Bring it to a heat and cook until the potatoes are juicy but not mushy, about 10-15 minutes. Drain and let them cool to room temperature.
2. Whisk together the mayonnaise, sour cream, white vinegar, Dijon mustard, and honey in a large mixing bowl. This dressing will be the heart of your potato salad.
3. Gingerly mix the cooled potatoes into the dressing, ensuring they are generously coated. This step permits the flavors to meld and infuse into the potatoes—season with your desired amount of pepper and salt.
4. Add the finely chopped dill pickles, minced red onion, and fresh dill to the potato mixture. The pickles bring a zesty crunch, while the dill provides a burst of fresh herbaceousness.
5. Cover the bowl with plastic wrap once all the ingredients are combined, and refrigerate for at least an hour. This resting period allows the flavors to develop and create a harmonious blend.
6. Before serving, give the potato salad a final stir to ensure an even distribution of the ingredients. Taste and adjust the seasoning if necessary.

Nutritional Information (Per Serving):

Calories: 324
Protein: 3g
Carbohydrates: 33g
Fat: 20g

Chapter 4: Hygge Desserts

Traditional Danish Rice Pudding (Risalamande)

The classic, comforting dish of Traditional Danish Rice Pudding, also known as Risalamande, embodies the essence of Hygge during the festive Christmas season. This heartwarming dessert invites you to savor the simple joys of life and bask in the warm embrace of tradition.

Creamy rice, subtly sweetened, is the base for this timeless treat, which boasts a delightful surprise hidden within. As you spoon into a serving of Risalamande, you'll uncover a whole almond, symbolizing good fortune and a yearning for togetherness.

Traditionally served with a dollop of cherry sauce, this dessert epitomizes Danish coziness, making it a must-have at your holiday gatherings. Share in the joy of creating cherished memories with a dish that encapsulates the true spirit of Christmas Hygge.

Yield: 4 Servings

Ingredients:

- 1 cup (250g/8.8 oz.) Arborio rice
- 2 cups (500ml/16.9 fl oz.) whole milk
- ½ a cup (125ml/4.2 fl oz.) heavy cream
- ½ a cup (125g/4.4 oz) granulated sugar
- One vanilla pod, split, and seeds scraped (or one teaspoon of vanilla extract)
- ¼ teaspoon (1.42g)(0.05 oz) of salt
- ½ a cup (125g/4.4 oz.) blanched almonds, finely chopped
- 1 ½ cups (375ml/12.7 fl oz.) cold whipping cream
- ¼ cup (30g/1.05 oz.) powdered sugar
- 1 cup (250ml/8.5 fl oz.) cherry compote or sauce
- One whole almond (with skin)

Instructions:

1. Begin by rinsing the Arborio rice under cold water. Drain and set it aside.
2. Combine the milk, heavy cream, granulated sugar, vanilla seeds (or extract), and a pinch of salt in a medium to large saucepan. Place it over medium-low heat, stirring from time to time until the mixture simmers.
3. Add the rinsed rice to the simmering mixture, reduce the heat to low, and let it cook gently for about 35-40 minutes, or until the rice is juicy and the mixture thickens, stirring occasionally to prevent sticking.
4. While the rice pudding is cooking, finely chop the blanched almonds and set them aside.
5. Once the rice is tender and the pudding has thickened, take off from the heat and allow it to cool to room temperature.
6. As the rice pudding cools, whip the cold whipping cream with powdered sugar until smooth peaks form.

7. Gently fold the chopped almonds and the whipped cream into the cooled rice pudding, ensuring a uniform, creamy texture.
8. Carefully insert the whole almond into the mixture, ensuring it's well hidden.
9. Transfer the Risalamande to the refrigerator and let it chill for at least 2 hours.
10. To serve, spoon the chilled rice pudding into individual serving bowls. Top with a generous dollop of cherry compote or sauce, and enjoy the festive fusion of flavors.

Nutritional Information (Per Serving):

Calories: 420
Protein: 8g
Carbohydrates: 45g
Fat: 24g

Gingerbread Cookies with Royal Icing

Indulge in the cozy and comforting embrace of the Christmas season with these Gingerbread Cookies adorned in delicate Royal Icing. A perfect embodiment of Hygge, these cookies bring the essence of coziness to your holiday festivities.

With their rich, spiced aroma and sweet, intricate designs, they will infuse your home with the spirit of the season. Prepare to create cherished memories and share the joy of the holidays with each delicious, hand-decorated bite.

Yield: 36 Cookies

Ingredients:

For the Gingerbread Cookies:

- 2 ¼ cups (531.3g/18.7 oz.) plain flour
- (2.5g)(0.09 oz.) or ½ teaspoon of ground cinnamon
- 1 ½ teaspoons (7.5g)(0.3 oz.) of ground ginger
- ½ teaspoon (2.5g)(0.09 oz.) of ground cloves
- ½ teaspoon (2.5g)(0.09 oz.) of baking soda
- ¼ teaspoon (1.42g)(0.05 oz.) of salt
- ½ a cup (125g/4.4 oz.) unsalted butter, softened
- ½ a cup (125g/4.4 oz.) brown sugar, packed
- ¼ cup (60ml/2.03 fl oz.) molasses
- One large egg

For the Royal Icing:

- 1 cup (250g/8.82 oz.) powdered sugar
- 1 ½ tablespoons (18g)(0.6 oz.) meringue powder
- Three tablespoons (45ml)(1.5 fl oz.) of warm water
- Food coloring (optional)

Instructions:

For the Gingerbread Cookies:

1. Whisk the flour, cinnamon, ginger, cloves, salt, and baking soda together in a medium-sized bowl. Set this dry mixture aside.
2. Cream the sugar and softened butter in a separate large dish until the gingerbread cookie mixture becomes light and fluffy.
3. Add the molasses and egg to the butter-sugar mixture, stirring until well combined.
4. Slowly mix the dry with the wet mixture, stirring until a dough forms. Be careful not to overmix.
5. Divide the dough in half, then shape each half into a disk. Wrap them slowly in plastic wrap and cool them for about 1 hour.
6. Heat your oven up to 350°F (180°C) and lay a baking sheet with enough baking paper.

7. Roll out the cooled dough on a floured surface to about 1/4 inch (0.6cm) thickness. Use gingerbread-shaped cookie cutters to cut out the cookies.
8. Place all the cookies on the prepared baking sheet, leaving some space between each one.
9. Bake in the oven for around 8-10 minutes or until the edges are lightly browned.
10. Allow the cookies to cool down on a cooling rack before decorating.

For the Royal Icing:

1. In a mixing dish, combine the powdered sugar and meringue powder.
2. Add warm water gradually, mixing until the icing reaches a thick but pipable consistency. If you'd like to use different colors, divide the icing into separate dishes and add food coloring as desired.
3. Transfer the icing to a piping or plastic food bag with a tiny hole cut in the corner.
4. Decorate the cooled gingerbread cookies as you wish with the royal icing. Let your creativity flow!

Nutritional Information (Per Serving):

Calories: 120
Protein: 1g
Carbohydrates: 22g
Fat: 3g

Cinnamon and Cardamom-Spiced Apple Pie

Get ready to embrace the cozy charm of the Christmas season with a warm, fragrant, and utterly comforting Cinnamon and Cardamom-Spiced Apple Pie. This classic dessert is a heartfelt invitation to experience the Danish concept of Hygge, where simple pleasures reign supreme.

As you savor each delicious bite, you'll find yourself wrapped in the soothing aroma of spices and tender apples' sweet, familiar taste. This recipe encapsulates the essence of togetherness and warmth, making it the perfect addition to your holiday celebrations. As you follow this easy and inviting recipe, prepare to create a little Hygge magic in your home.

Yield: 8 Servings

Ingredients:

For the Apple Pie Crust:

- 2 ½ cups (625g/22 oz.) plain flour
- 1 cup (250g/8.82 oz.) cold unsalted butter, cubed
- One teaspoon (5g) (0.18 oz.) sugar
- ½ a teaspoon salt (2.5g)(0.09 oz.)
- 6-8 tablespoons ice-cold water(90-120ml)(3.04-4.06 fl oz.)

For the Apple Pie Filling:

- 6-8 medium-sized apples (about 2 ½ pounds or 1.2kg), a mix of Granny Smith and Honeycrisp, peeled, cored, and sliced thinly
- ¾ cup (150g/5.29 oz.) granulated sugar
- 2 tablespoons (28.3g)(1 oz.) plain flour
- One teaspoon (5g) (0.18 oz.) of ground cinnamon
- ½ a teaspoon (2.5g)(0.09 oz.) of ground cardamom
- ¼ teaspoon (1.42g)(0.05 oz.) of salt
- One tablespoon (15ml)(0.5 fl oz.) of lemon juice

For the Topping:

- One egg, beaten (for egg wash)
- One tablespoon (15ml)(0.5 fl oz.) of granulated sugar mixed with ½ a teaspoon (2.5g)(0.09 oz.) of ground cinnamon (for sprinkling)

Instructions:

For the Apple Pie Crust:

1. Combine the sugar, salt, and flour in a medium to large mixing bowl.
2. Now incorporate the cold, cubed butter and use your fingers or a pastry cutter to work it into the dry ingredients until the pie crust mixture looks similar to coarse crumbs.
3. Slowly add the chilled water, one tablespoon (15ml)(0.5 fl oz.) at a time, and mix it enough until the pie crust dough comes together. Form it into two discs, wrap them in a wrap, and cool in the refrigerator for about 30 minutes.

For the Apple Pie Filling:

1. Heat up your oven to 425°F (220°C).
2. In a large dish, incorporate the sugar, sliced apples, flour, cinnamon, cardamom, salt, and lemon juice. Toss until the apples are lovely and evenly coated with the mixture.

Assembling the Pie:

1. Roll out a cooled pie crust on a floured surface to fit a (23cm) or 9-inch pie dish. Place it in the container, trimming any excess overhang.
2. Fill the apple pie crust with the spiced apple mixture, creating a slight mound in the middle.
3. Roll out the second apple pie crust and place it over the apples. Trim away any excess and crimp the pastry edges to seal the apple pie.
4. Cut a few decorative slits on the top crust to let steam escape.
5. Brush the top part of the crust using the egg wash or beaten egg mixture, then sprinkle the cinnamon-sugar mixture evenly.

Baking the Pie:

1. Place the whole apple pie on a flat baking sheet to catch anything that drips, and bake in your gas or convection oven for around 45-50 minutes or until you see a fully golden crust and the filling is clearly bubbling.
2. Cover the pie edges with aluminum foil if they begin to brown too quickly.
3. Allow the apple pie to come to room temperature for a minimum of 2 hours before serving. This allows the filling to set.

Nutritional Information (Per Serving):

Calories: 384
Protein: 3g
Carbohydrates: 54g
Fat: 17g

Chocolate Peppermint Bark

Indulge in the comforting embrace of the holiday season with our exquisite Chocolate Peppermint Bark. This delightful confection perfectly embodies Hygge, offering warmth and coziness to your Christmas celebrations.

Crafted with simple ingredients and a touch of love, this recipe promises to wrap you in a snug, familiar embrace. It's a quintessential treat that captures the essence of a Hygge Christmas, inviting you to savor each bite with a cup of hot cocoa and a cozy blanket. So, let's embark on this culinary journey and create a little moment of warmth and togetherness this holiday season.

Yield: +-24 servings

Ingredients:

- 12 ounces (340.2g) dark chocolate (70% cocoa or higher)
- 12 ounces (340.2g) white chocolate
- One teaspoon (5g) (0.18 oz.) of peppermint extract
- 3-4 candy canes, crushed
- A pinch of salt

Instructions:

1. Begin by preparing a baking sheet or tray and lining it with parchment paper. This will make it easier to remove the bark later.
2. Liquefy the dark chocolate in a microwave-safe dish, using 20-30-second intervals, stirring between intervals until smooth. You may also use a double boiler for this part if you prefer.
3. Once the dark chocolate is smooth, stir in half the peppermint extract and a pinch of salt.
4. This will enhance the depth of flavor and provide a lovely contrast to the sweetness.
5. Pour the dark chocolate slowly onto the baking paper, spreading it evenly to create a creamy layer. It must be about 1/4 inch thick.
6. Allow the dark chocolate to set for about 20-30 minutes or until slightly firm.
7. While the dark chocolate is slowly setting, melt the white chocolate using the exact same method you used for the dark chocolate. Mix in the remaining half of the peppermint extract.
8. Once the dark chocolate layer is slightly firm, pour the melted white chocolate over it, creating an even layer.
9. Before the white chocolate fully sets, sprinkle the crushed candy canes evenly over the top. Gently press them into the white chocolate so they stick.
10. Let the bark set at room temperature until completely firm, which should take about 2-3 hours.
11. Once the Chocolate Peppermint Bark is firm, use a knife to break it into irregular, rustic pieces.

Nutritional Information (Per Serving):

Calories: 140
Protein: 1g
Carbohydrates: 16g
Fat: 8g

Danish Kringle Pastry with Almonds and Cinnamon

Indulge in the comforting warmth of the Christmas season with our Danish Kringle Pastry. A delightful blend of almonds and cinnamon come together perfectly, making this pastry a cherished holiday treat.

This recipe embraces the essence of Hygge, inviting you to savor every bite with a sense of cozy contentment. Join us as we guide you through the simple steps to create this delectable delight that embodies the true spirit of Christmas.

Yield: 8 Servings

Ingredients:

- Two sheets of puff pastry (9x9 inches / 23x23 cm)
- 1 cup (250g/8.8 oz.) ground almonds
- ¼ cup (60g/2.01 oz.) granulated sugar
- 1 teaspoon(5g) (0.18 oz.) of ground cinnamon
- ½ a cup (125g)(4.4 oz.) unsalted butter, softened
- One egg, beaten (for egg wash)
- ¼ cup (60g/2.1 oz.) powdered sugar (for dusting)
- Sliced almonds for garnish (optional)

Instructions:

1. Heat up your oven to 375°F (190°C).
2. Combine the ground almonds, granulated sugar, and cinnamon in a mixing bowl. Mix well to create the almond-cinnamon filling.
3. Lay out a single sheet of puff pastry on a baking sheet lined with any baking paper.
4. Spread out half of the softened butter evenly over the pastry sheet.
5. Sprinkle the almond-cinnamon filling evenly over the buttered pastry sheet.
6. Place the second sheet of puff pastry on top of the filling and press the edges gently to seal. Brush the top with the beaten egg for a golden finish.
7. Bake in your oven for 20-25 minutes or until the pastry is golden brown and puffed up.
8. Allow the Danish Kringle to cool briefly before transferring it to a wire rack.
9. Once the pastry has cooled, dust it with powdered sugar for sweetness. You can also sprinkle sliced almonds for extra texture and flavor.

10. Slice the Kringle into servings, and serve it with a hot cup of brewed coffee or hot cocoa to fully embrace the Hygge spirit.

Nutritional Information (Per Serving):

Calories: 380
Protein: 6g
Carbohydrates: 33g
Fat: 26g

Chapter 5:Sweet Hygge Treats

Homemade Hot Chocolate with Whipped Cream

Indulge in the heartwarming comfort of a cozy Christmas tradition with our Homemade Hot Chocolate with Whipped Cream. This delightful beverage encapsulates the essence of Hygge, embracing simplicity and the pleasure of the present moment.

As you sip on this velvety elixir, you'll find yourself wrapped in a soothing embrace of rich cocoa and the cloud-like perfection of freshly whipped cream. It's a familiar and cherished recipe that invites you to unwind and savor the warmth of the holiday season.

Yield: 2 Cups

Ingredients:

- 2 cups (500 ml/16.16 fl oz) whole milk
- ½ a cup (125 ml/4.06 fl oz) cream heavy
- ¼ cup (30 g/1.05 oz) cocoa powder unsweetened
- ¼ cup (50 g/1.76 oz) granulated sugar
- ½ a cup (125 g/3.17 oz) chocolate chips semi-sweet
- ½ a (2.5 ml/0.08 fl oz) teaspoon vanilla extract
- A pinch of salt

For the Whipped Cream:

- 1 cup (250ml/8.4 fl oz.) heavy cream
- Two (30ml/1 oz) tablespoons powdered sugar
- ½ (2.5ml/ 0.08 fl oz.) teaspoon vanilla extract

Instructions:

1. In a medium-sized saucepan, combine the whole milk, heavy cream, unsweetened cocoa powder, granulated sugar, semi-sweet chocolate chips, and a pinch of salt. Place it over low heat.
2. Stir steadily with a whisk until the mixture is smooth and the chocolate completely melts. It should take about 5-7 minutes. Do not let it boil.
3. Once everything is well combined, remove the saucepan from the stovetop and slowly stir in the vanilla extract. Your velvety hot chocolate base is ready.
4. In a separate dish, make the whipped cream. Pour the heavy cream into a cooled mixing dish and add powdered sugar and vanilla extract. Whip with an electric blender on medium-high speed until soft peaks form. This should take about 2-3 minutes.
5. To serve, spoon the hot chocolate into mugs, leaving some space for the whipped cream at the top.

6. Spoon a generous dollop of the freshly whipped cream on top of each mug of hot chocolate.
7. For that extra touch of holiday cheer, you can sprinkle a dash of cocoa powder or chocolate shavings over the whipped cream.

Nutritional Information (Per Serving): 1 Cup/250ml/8.4 fl oz.

Calories: 450
Protein: 6g
Carbohydrates: 34g
Fat: 34g

Danish æbleskiver (Apple Pancake Puffs)

Danish æbleskiver, also known as Apple Pancake Puffs, is a delightful and cozy treat that captures the essence of Hygge during Christmas. These round, fluffy delights are perfect for creating warm, comforting moments. The familiar aroma of apples and the soft, tender texture of these puffs make them a cherished part of the holiday season.

This recipe is perfect for a cozy Christmas gathering brimming with Hygge. Enjoy the heartwarming sensation these delightful treats bring, sharing the love and comfort of the holiday season with friends and family. Join us as we explore this simple yet heartwarming recipe that brings the Danish tradition of Hygge to your Christmas table.

Yield: 4 Servings

Ingredients:

- 1 cup (250ml/8.4 fl oz.) buttermilk
- Two large eggs
- One teaspoon of vanilla extract (5ml/0.16 fl oz.)
- One tablespoon of granulated sugar (15 g/0.5 oz.)
- One teaspoon of ground cinnamon (5g/0.16 oz.)
- ½ a teaspoon baking powder (2.5g/0.08oz.)
- ½ a teaspoon baking soda (2.5g/0.08 oz.)
- ¼ teaspoon salt (12.5g/0.25 oz.)
- 1 ½ cups (375g/ 13.22 oz.) of plain flour
- Two apples (peeled, cored, and finely diced)
- Butter or oil for greasing the Æbleskiver pan

Dipping Suggestions:

- Powdered sugar
- Raspberry jam
- Caramel sauce

Instructions:

1. Whisk together eggs, vanilla extract, and buttermilk in a mixing bowl until well combined.

2. Mix sugar, ground cinnamon, baking powder, salt, all-purpose, and baking powder flour in a separate bowl. Slowly combine this wet mixture with the dry ingredients, stirring until a smooth batter forms.
3. Gently fold the diced apples, ensuring an even distribution throughout the batter.
4. Place an Æbleskiver pan on medium heat and grease each well with butter or oil.
5. Fill each well with a spoonful of the apple-infused batter, ensuring they are about 3/4 full.
6. Allow them to cook until the edges set and turn golden, typically taking 3-4 minutes. Use a skewer or fork to flip them over, letting the other side cook until golden.
7. Transfer the Danish Æbleskiver to a serving plate. They should be perfectly puffed, crispy on the outside, and delightfully moist on the inside.

To Serve:

Dust the warm Æbleskiver with powdered sugar for a touch of sweetness, or serve with a side of raspberry jam or caramel sauce for a delightful contrast.

Nutritional Information (Per Serving): +-4 Æbleskiver

Calories: 220
Carbohydrates: 36g
Protein: 6g
Fat: 6g

Spiced Scandinavian Glogg

In the heart of the Christmas season, what better way to embrace the cozy concept of Hygge than with a warm and aromatic cup of Spiced Scandinavian Glogg? This traditional Nordic beverage is a soothing blend of spices and red wine, creating an inviting ambiance that captures the essence of a Scandinavian winter. Let's delve into this timeless recipe, guaranteed to bring comfort and cheer to your holiday gatherings.

Yield: 6-8 Servings

Ingredients:

- 750ml (3 cups/ 25.36 fl oz.) red wine
- 1 cup (250ml/ 8.4 fl oz.) port wine

- 1 cup (250 ml/8.4 fl oz.) brandy
- Two cinnamon sticks
- Six cloves
- Six cardamom pods, crushed
- One orange peel, grated
- One lemon peel, grated
- ½ a cup (125g/4.41 oz.) brown sugar
- ⅓ cup (75g/2.75 oz.) raisins
- ⅓ cup (75g/2.75 oz.) blanched almonds
- 1-star anise
- One vanilla bean, split and scraped
- Two slices of fresh ginger
- One black peppercorn
- Pinch of nutmeg
- Pinch of dried currants
- Pinch of dried apricots

Instructions:

1. Combine the red wine, port wine, and brandy in a large saucepan. Place it over low heat and let it warm gently without boiling.
2. Add the cinnamon sticks, cloves, cardamom pods, orange peel, lemon peel, brown sugar, raisins, and blanched almonds to the pot. Stir well to combine.
3. Carefully split the vanilla bean, scrape out the seeds, and add the roots and the bean to the mixture.
4. Drop in the star anise, slices of fresh ginger, black peppercorn, and a pinch of nutmeg.
5. Let the mixture simmer for 20-25 minutes, melding the flavors together. Do not boil the mix; you want it hot enough to steep the spices.
6. Before serving, strain the glogg into mugs or heatproof glasses. Add a few dried currants and apricots to each serving, letting them soak up the warm, spiced liquid.
7. Serve the Spiced Scandinavian Glogg while still hot, and enjoy the cozy ambiance it creates.

Nutritional Information (Per Serving): 1 Cup/250ml/8.4 fl oz.

Calories: 180
Protein: 0.5g
Carbohydrates: 15g
Fat: 1g

Sugar-Coated Almonds (Brændte Mandler)

Indulge in the cozy embrace of the Christmas season with this delightful treat, Sugar-Coated Almonds, known as Brændte Mandler. These sweet, crunchy morsels bring comfort and warmth to your holiday gatherings, embodying the essence of Hygge. Embrace the simple pleasure of toasty almonds enveloped in a sugary embrace, offering a delightful contrast of flavors and textures.

A perfect choice for a cup of hot cocoa or a cozy evening by the fireplace, this recipe will become a cherished part of your festive traditions. Prepare to savor the heartwarming essence of Brændte Mandler, the epitome of Hygge, during the Christmas season.

Yields: 2 Cups

Ingredients:

- 1 cup (250g/8.46 oz.) white sugar
- 119ml (4.02 fl oz.) of water
- 1 (15g/0.5 oz) tablespoon cinnamon
- 2 cups of almonds (500g/16.93 oz.)

Instructions:

1. Spread a parchment-lined tray for your culinary canvas.
2. In a saucepan over medium to low heat, let sugar, water, and cinnamon fuse in a fragrant concoction until it sizzles. Introduce the almonds to the dance, stirring until the transformation is complete, leaving behind a glossy sheen.
3. Now, place the sweetened almonds onto the awaiting parchment stage, enlisting two forks to gracefully unravel any gatherings, creating a harmonious almond tapestry. Grant them a brief interlude to cool, approximately 15 minutes.

Nutrition Information: (Per Serving): 1 Cup/250ml/8.4 fl oz.

Calories: 304
Protein: 8g
Carbohydrates: 33g
Fat: 18g

Cardamom Buns (Kardemummabullar)

Cardamom buns, known as kardemummabullar in Swedish, are a traditional Scandinavian pastry. They are made with yeast dough and flavored with ground cardamom, which gives them a distinctive sweet and spicy flavor, making it perfect for a small gathering or keeping a batch on hand for quiet, comforting moments.

These buns are often served with powdered sugar and are a popular treat in Sweden and other Scandinavian countries during the holiday season. Enjoy these Cardamom Buns, each bite filled with the rich aroma of cardamom and the warmth of Hygge.

Yield: 12 Buns

Ingredients:

For the Dough:

- 250g (1 ¾ cups/8.87 oz.) plain flour
- 50g (1/4 cup/1.76 oz.) granulated sugar
- 5g (1 ½ tsp/0.17 oz.) active dry yeast
- 150ml (2/3 cup/5.07 fl oz.) whole milk
- 40g (3 tbsp/1.41 oz.) unsalted butter, melted
- ½ a tsp (2.5g/0.85 oz)cardamom seeds, crushed
- A pinch of salt

For the Filling:

- 40g (1/3 cup/1.41 oz.) granulated sugar
- 1 ½ tsp(7.5g/0.25 oz.) ground cardamom
- 60g (1/4 cup/2.10 oz.) unsalted butter, softened

For the Glaze:

- One egg, beaten
- A handful of pearl sugar (or crushed sugar cubes)

Instructions:

1. Begin by warming the milk until it's lukewarm. Mix in the yeast and let it rest for a few minutes until it becomes frothy.
2. Combine the flour, sugar, crushed cardamom seeds, and a pinch of salt in a large mixing dish. Merge the melted butter and the yeast mixture to the dry ingredients. Mix until a soft dough forms.
3. Put the dough onto a floured surface and knead it for about 5-7 minutes until it turns smooth and elastic. Place the dough back into the dish, cover it with kitchen paper, and allow it to rise in a warmish place for about 1 hour or until it's doubled.
4. While the dough rises, prepare the cardamom filling by mixing the softened butter, ground cardamom, and sugar in a small bowl until it forms a smooth, fragrant paste.
5. Once the dough has doubled, punch it down and roll it into a large rectangle on a floured surface.

6. Spread the cardamom filling over the dough, leaving a small border along one edge. Roll up the dough tightly, beginning from the opposite edge. Slice the roll into 12 equal pieces.
7. Place the buns onto a grease-proof lined baking tray, close them, and let them rise for 30 minutes.
8. Heat your oven to around 200°C (392°F).
9. Before baking, brush the buns with the beaten egg and sprinkle them with pearl sugar.
10. Bake for 15-20 minutes until golden brown and sounds hollow when tapped on the bottom.
11. Allow the buns to cool before placing them on a wire rack before serving.

Nutritional Information (Per Serving): 1 Bun

Calories: 220
Protein: 4g
Carbohydrates: 29g
Fat: 10g

Chapter 6: Hygge Cocktails and Beverages

Christmas Spiced Tea

This festive blend is a perfect addition to your holiday celebrations. It's warm and comforting and made with a mix of black tea, spices, and natural flavors, perfect for sharing the warmth and coziness of the holiday season with your loved ones.

Enjoy Christmas Spiced Tea's enchanting flavors and soothing aromas as you create cherished moments of Hygge this Christmas.

Pour yourself a mug and enjoy the warm, cozy feeling of sipping on Christmas Spiced Tea.

Yield: 8 Cups

Ingredients:

- 4 cups (1000ml/32.46 fl oz.) water
- Six whole cloves
- Two cinnamon sticks
- 3 star anise pods
- Two orange peels
- Four black tea bags
- ¼ cup (60ml/2.02 fl oz.) honey
- ¼ cup (60ml/2.02 fl oz.) brown sugar
- ½ a cup (125ml/4.05 fl oz.) apple cider
- ½ a cup (125ml/4.05 fl oz.) cranberry juice
- ½ a cup (125ml/4.05 fl oz.) orange juice
- ½ a teaspoon (2.5g/0.085 oz.) ground nutmeg
- ½ a teaspoon (2.5g/0.085 oz.) ground ginger
- ¼ teaspoon (1.25g/0.045 oz.) ground allspice
- ¼ teaspoon (1.25g/0.045 oz.) ground cardamom

Instructions:

1. Combine the water, cloves, cinnamon sticks, star anise, and orange peels in a large saucepan. Bring the blend to a gentle simmer over medium heat. Let it infuse for about 15 minutes.
2. Next, remove the saucepan from the stovetop and add the black tea bags. Allow the black tea to brew for 5 minutes or longer for a more robust flavor, according to your preference.
3. Discard the tea bags and the whole spices from the mixture.
4. Stir in the honey, brown sugar, apple cider, cranberry juice, orange juice, ground nutmeg, ginger, ground allspice, and ground cardamom. Return the saucepan to the stove and heat over medium-low heat, stirring occasionally, until the tea is heated and the flavors meld together.

5. Once heated to your liking, pour the Christmas Spiced Tea into mugs or teacups. Garnish each serving with a cinnamon stick or a slice of fresh orange, if desired.

Nutritional Information (Per Serving): 1 Cup/250ml/8.4 fl oz.

Calories: 105
Protein: 0g
Carbohydrates: 27g
Fat: 0g

Nordic-inspired Cranberry Punch

This refreshing drink is a perfect fit for the crisp autumn weather. The cranberry juice provides a tangy flavor, while the other ingredients provide a hint of sweetness and a subtle fruity taste. It's perfect for sipping on a cold evening or as a holiday party drink. Give it a try, and enjoy the Nordic twist, an ideal addition to your holiday gatherings, ensuring everyone can savor a taste of Nordic-inspired Hygge this Christmas.

Yield: +-6 Cups

Ingredients:

- 4 cups (1000ml/32.12 fl oz.) cranberry juice
- 1 cup (250ml/8.11 fl oz.) apple cider
- ½ a cup (125ml/4.05 fl oz.) orange juice
- ¼ cup (60ml/2.02 fl oz.) honey
- Two cinnamon sticks
- Four whole cloves
- 1 star anise
- One orange, thinly sliced
- One lemon, thinly sliced
- 1 cup (250ml/8.11 fl oz.) sparkling water (optional)
- Fresh cranberries and rosemary sprigs for garnish

Instructions:

1. Combine cranberry juice, orange juice, and apple cider in a large saucepan. Stir in honey and place the saucepan over medium heat. Allow it to heat gently, stirring occasionally, until the mixture is just about to simmer. Do not boil.
2. Reduce the heat to low and add the cinnamon sticks, cloves, and star anise. Let the punch simmer gently for about 15-20 minutes, allowing the spices to infuse their warm, comforting aromas.
3. While the punch is simmering, prepare your serving glasses. Place a slice of orange and lemon in each glass.
4. Remove it from the heat once the punch has simmered and the flavors have melded beautifully. Depending on your preference, you can strain it to remove the spices or leave them in for a more robust flavor.

5. Spoon the warm cranberry punch into the prepared glasses. If you like, add a splash of sparkling water for a touch of enthusiasm.
6. Garnish your Nordic-inspired Cranberry Punch with fresh cranberries and a sprig of rosemary for that extra festive touch.
7. Serve your punch warm and relish in its inviting blend of flavors. Enjoy the companionship and warmth this delightful beverage brings during the Christmas season.

Nutritional Information (Per Serving, Without Sparkling Water): 1 Cup/250ml/8.4 fl oz.

Calories: 120
Protein: 0.5g
Carbohydrates: 31g
Fat: 0g

Warm Cider with Mulled Spices

Warm Cider with Mulled Spices is a popular fall drink made with apple cider, sugar, and a mixture of heating spices such as cinnamon, nutmeg, and cloves. The herbs are added to the cider and simmered to create a flavorful and comforting drink perfect for cool fall evenings and sharing the Hygge spirit during Christmas. Enjoy the delightful warmth and camaraderie this heartening cider brings to your festivities.

Yield: 4 Cups

Ingredients:

- 4 cups (1000ml/31.98 fl oz.) of apple cider
- Two cinnamon sticks

- Five whole cloves
- Three allspice berries
- 1 star anise
- Two slices of fresh orange peel
- ¼ cup (50g/1.76 oz.) of brown sugar (adjust to taste)
- ¼ teaspoon(0.25g/0.041 oz.) of grated nutmeg
- ¼ teaspoon(0.25g/0.041 oz.) of ground ginger
- Whipped cream, for garnish (optional)
- Orange slices and cinnamon sticks for garnish (optional)

Instructions:

1. In a medium-sized saucepan, pour the apple cider and place it over medium heat.
2. Add the cinnamon sticks, whole cloves, allspice berries, star anise, and fresh orange peel to the cider. Stir gently to combine.
3. Sprinkle in the brown sugar and add the grated nutmeg and ground ginger. These delightful spices will infuse the cider with a cozy warmth.
4. Bring the cider to a gentle simmer, then reduce the heat to low. Let it gently bubble away, allowing the flavors to meld, for about 15-20 minutes. Stir occasionally.
5. Remove it from the heat once the cider has absorbed the aromatic spices and takes on a rich, mulled fragrance.
6. Strain the warm cider into mugs or heatproof glasses, discarding the spices and orange peel.
7. Serve your Warm Cider with Mulled Spices piping hot. You can top it with a dollop of whipped cream, an orange slice, or a cinnamon stick for an extra charm.

Nutritional Information (Per Serving): 1 Cup/250ml/8.4 fl oz.

Calories: 145
Protein: 0g
Carbohydrates: 36g
Fat: 0g

Scandinavian Aquavit for Toasting

Scandinavian Aquavit is a traditional spirit typically made from potatoes, barley, or wheat and flavored with herbs and spices such as dill, caraway, and fennel. It is commonly used for toasting during special occasions in Scandinavian culture. It is known for its crisp, clean taste and subtle flavor profile, making it perfect for sharing the warmth of the holiday season with friends and family. Skål (Cheers)!

Yield: +-25 Shots

Ingredients:

- One bottle (750 ml/25.36 fl oz.) of high-quality vodka (40% alcohol)
- Ten whole caraway seeds

- Five whole fennel seeds
- Two whole dill seeds
- Two whole coriander seeds
- One small strip of lemon or orange zest (about 2 inches long)
- One small strip of cucumber peel (about 2 inches long)
- One small strip of apple peel (about 2 inches long)
- One small strip of fresh ginger (about 2 inches long)
- One small clove of garlic, peeled
- One whole star anise
- One small cinnamon stick
- One small cardamom pod
- One small bay leaf
- One small juniper berry
- One small sprig of fresh thyme
- One small sprig of fresh rosemary
- One small sprig of fresh dill
- One small sprig of fresh parsley
- One small pinch of black peppercorns

Instructions:

1. Begin by gently toasting the caraway, fennel, dill, and coriander seeds in a clean and dry cast iron skillet over low heat. Toast them until they release their aromatic flavors, but be careful not to burn them. This should take about 1-2 minutes.
2. In a clean glass mason jar or airtight container, add the toasted seeds, lemon or orange zest, cucumber peel, apple peel, ginger, garlic, star anise, cinnamon stick, cardamom pod, bay leaf, juniper berry, thyme, rosemary, dill, parsley, and black peppercorns.
3. Pour the vodka into the jar, ensuring all the ingredients are fully submerged. Seal the jar tightly.
4. Store the jar in a cool, dark place for at least 48 hours, allowing the flavors to meld and infuse. Some enthusiasts prefer a more extended infusion, up to a week, for a richer taste.

5. Once the infusion is complete, strain the Aquavit through a cheesecloth or fine-mesh sieve straight into a clean bottle, removing all the solid ingredients.
6. Seal the bottle and let it rest for another day or two to harmonize the flavors further.

To Serve:

Chill your homemade Scandinavian Aquavit in the freezer for a few hours before serving. It's traditionally served in small, ice-cold shot glasses, encouraging you to savor its exquisite flavor while toasting to the season's joy.

Nutritional Information (Per Serving): 1 Shot/45ml/1.52 fl oz

Calories: 120
Protein: 0g
Carbohydrates: 0g
Fat: 0g

Creamy Irish Coffee

A delicious and rich cocktail that's perfect for cold winter nights. This drink will warm your soul and is made with whiskey, coffee, sugar, and whipped cream, making it the ideal winter warmer for those seeking a festive Irish Hygge.

Enjoy the heartwarming tradition of a well-crafted Irish coffee, perfect for sipping and savoring on Christmas Eve or any cozy evening by the hearth. If you're feeling extra festive, try topping it with a sprinkle of nutmeg for an added magic touch. So go ahead, indulge in this creamy delight, and toast to the holiday season!

Yield: 1 Cup

Ingredients:

- 1 cup (250ml/8.4 fl oz.) hot brewed coffee
- 1.52 fl oz. (45ml) Irish whiskey
- Two tablespoons (30ml/1.01 fl oz.) brown sugar
- Two tablespoons (30ml/1.01 fl oz.) heavy cream
- Whipped cream, for garnish
- Grated nutmeg for garnish

Instructions:

1. Freshly brew your favorite coffee and pour it into a heatproof glass or mug.
2. Add the Irish whiskey to the hot coffee and brown sugar. Stir nicely until the sugar is fully dissolved.
3. To create the creamy topping, carefully pour the heavy cream over the back of a spoon just above the coffee's surface. This will help it float on top, creating that luxurious layer.
4. For an extra touch of Hygge comfort, add a small amount of whipped cream on top of the creamy layer.
5. Next, dusting freshly grated nutmeg adds a touch of warmth and spice. Sprinkle it over the whipped cream.
6. Serve your Creamy Irish Coffee immediately, savoring its comforting flavors and the harmonious blend of textures.

Nutritional Information (Per Serving): 1 Cup/250ml/8.4 fl oz.

Calories: 210
Protein: 1g
Carbohydrates: 18g
Fat: 6g

Chapter 7: Hygge Leftovers

Turkey and Cranberry Sandwich with Stuffing

Wallow in the warm and comforting embrace of Hygge this Christmas season with our delightful Turkey and Cranberry Sandwich with Stuffing. This recipe marries the richness of roasted turkey, the sweet tang of cranberry sauce, and the hearty goodness of stuffing, all enclosed in a cozy, satisfying sandwich that captures the essence of festive bliss. Perfect for a leisurely holiday brunch, this recipe will leave you and your loved ones feeling snug and content.

Servings: 4 Sandwiches

Ingredients:

For the Roasted Turkey:

- 1 Pound (450g/15.87 oz.) boneless turkey breast
- Two tablespoons(30ml/1 fl oz.) of olive oil
- One teaspoon(5ml/0.16 oz.) of dried sage
- Salt and black pepper to your desired taste

For the Cranberry Sauce:

- 1 cup (250g/8.46 oz.) cranberries (fresh or frozen)
- ½ a cup (125g/3.52 oz.) granulated sugar
- ½ a cup (125ml/3.4 fl oz.) water
- One teaspoon(5g/0.16 oz.) of orange zest

For the Stuffing:

- 4 cups (1000g/14.10 oz.) cubed bread (white or whole-grain)
- Two tablespoons(30g/1 oz.) unsalted butter
- One small onion, finely chopped
- Two cloves garlic, minced
- One celery stalk, finely chopped
- ½ a teaspoon(2.5g/0.25 oz.) dried thyme
- ½ a teaspoon(2.5g/0.25 oz.) dried rosemary
- Salt and black pepper to your desired taste
- 1 cup (250ml/8.1 fl oz.) chicken or vegetable broth

For the Sandwich Assembly:

- Eight slices of your favorite bread (rye, sourdough, or white)
- ¼ cup (60ml/2.02 fl oz.) mayonnaise
- Four lettuce leaves
- 1 cup (250g/8.4 oz.) arugula or baby spinach
- Four slices of Swiss or cheddar cheese

Instructions:

Roasting Turkey:

- Preheat your gas or convection oven to 375°F (190°C). Rub the turkey breast with olive oil, dried sage, salt, and pepper. Place the seasoned whole turkey into a roasting pan and roast for approximately 25-30 minutes or until the turkey's internal temperature reaches 165°F (74°C). Remove the roasted turkey from the oven, let it rest for 10 minutes, and then slice into thin pieces.

Cranberry Sauce:

- In a medium-sized saucepan, combine sugar, cranberries, water, and orange zest. Bring to a heat, then reduce the heat and simmer for 10-12 minutes until the simmering cranberries burst and the cranberry sauce begins to thicken. Let it cool.

Making the Stuffing:

- In a large frying pan, soften the butter over medium heat. Add chopped onion, garlic, and celery, and sauté until they become tender. Stir in dried thyme, dried rosemary, salt, and black pepper. Add cubed bread and toss to combine. Pour the chicken or vegetable broth and mix well until the stuffing is moist but not soggy.

Sandwich Assembly:

- Lay out eight slices of fresh bread and spread mayonnaise on one side of each slice. On four slices, layer lettuce, roasted turkey slices, cranberry sauce, stuffing, arugula or spinach, and a slice of cheese. Top up with the remaining bread slices, mayonnaise side down.

Serving:

- Cut each sandwich in half diagonally. Serve warm and embrace the cozy Hygge vibes of this festive delight.

Nutritional Information (Per Serving): 1 Sandwich

Calories: 620
Protein: 33g
Carbohydrates: 76g
Fat: 21g

Creamy Turkey and Wild Rice Soup

Creamy Turkey with Wild Rice Soup is a comforting and flavorful soup made with tender pieces of turkey, wild rice, and a rich, creamy broth, making it the perfect sharing dish for friends and family during the Christmas season, creating an atmosphere of warmth and togetherness.

It's the perfect dish for a chilly fall or winter evening and can be easily customized to suit your taste preferences. You can add celery, spinach, or carrots for nutrition and flavor.

Yield: 6 Servings

Ingredients:

- 2 cups (500ml/16.67 fl oz.) turkey leftovers, diced
- 1 cup (250g/6.34 oz.) wild rice
- 4 cups (1000ml/32.46 fl oz.) chicken broth
- 1 cup (250ml/8.4 fl oz.) heavy cream
- One medium onion, finely chopped
- Two cloves garlic, minced
- Two carrots, peeled and diced
- Two celery stalks, chopped
- Two tablespoons (30g/1.05 oz.) butter
- Two tablespoons (30g/1.05 oz.) plain flour
- One teaspoon (5g/0.17 oz.) dried thyme
- Salt and pepper, to taste
- Fresh parsley for garnish

Instructions:

1. In a large cooking utensil, melt the butter over medium heat. Add the chopped onion, garlic, carrots, and celery. Sauté until the vegetables are tender, about 5 minutes.
2. Stir in the plain flour and continue to cook for 2-3 minutes, stirring regularly, until it forms a light roux.
3. Pour in the chicken broth, mix to combine, and bring the mixture to a boil.
4. Add the wild rice, dried thyme, and a pinch of salt and pepper. Reduce the heat, cover, and cook gently for about 45 minutes or until the wild rice is tender.
5. Stir in the diced turkey leftovers and simmer for 10 minutes, allowing the flavors to fuse.
6. Pour in the heavy cream, stirring gently to create a lusciously creamy texture. Simmer for an additional 5 minutes.

7. Taste the soup and balance the seasonings with salt and pepper as needed.
8. Serve hot, garnished with fresh parsley for a pop of color and flavor.

Nutritional Information (Per Serving): 1 Soup Bowl

Calories: 320
Protein: 20g
Carbohydrates: 27g
Fat: 15g

Christmas Dinner Hash

This delicious dish is a popular alternative to traditional roasted turkey or ham on Christmas Day. It's a hearty mix of cooked vegetables, meat, and seasonings, often made with leftover roast dinner components.

Some common ingredients include potatoes, onions, carrots, peas, and bacon or sausage. Hash can be served as either a main course or as a side dish, making it a delightful choice for a cozy family gathering or a warm and inviting dinner for two during the holiday season.

Embrace the essence of Hygge with Christmas Dinner Hash, where cherished leftovers are transformed into a comforting and memorable meal that celebrates the true spirit of togetherness. It's sure to be a hit with your family and friends this holiday season.

Yield: 4 Servings

Ingredients:

- 2 cups (500g/16.06 fl oz.) diced roasted turkey or chicken
- 2 cups (500g/16.06 fl oz.) diced roasted potatoes
- 1 cup (250g/8.1 fl oz.) diced roasted carrots
- 1 cup (250g/8.1 fl oz.) diced roasted Brussels sprouts
- 1 cup (250g/8.1 fl oz.) diced roasted butternut squash
- 1 cup (250g/8.1 fl oz.) chopped roasted onions
- Two cloves of garlic, minced
- Two tablespoons (30ml/1.01 fl oz.) olive oil
- One teaspoon (5g/0.16 fl oz.) dried thyme
- One teaspoon (5g/0.16 fl oz.) dried rosemary
- Salt and black pepper to your desired taste
- Gravy or cranberry sauce (optional for serving)

Instructions:

Heat up your olive oil in a large frying pan over medium heat. Add the minced garlic and sauté for about 1 minute until fragrant.

1. Add the diced roasted onions to the skillet and sauté for 2-3 minutes until they become slightly caramelized.

2. Toss in the diced roasted turkey or chicken and continue to sauté for 3-4 minutes, allowing the meat to heat through.
3. Add the diced roasted potatoes, carrots, Brussels sprouts, and butternut squash to the skillet. Sprinkle the dried thyme and rosemary over the ingredients.
4. Stir well and cook for another 5-7 minutes, occasionally flipping the ingredients, until they start to crisp up and develop a golden brown hue.
5. Season with your desired amount of salt and black pepper.
6. Serve your Christmas Dinner Hash hot, with a drizzle of gravy or a dollop of cranberry sauce if desired.

Nutritional Information (Per Serving): 1 Bowl of Hash

Calories: 375
Protein: 23g
Carbohydrates: 45g
Fat: 12g

Leftover Dessert Parfait

A Leftover Dessert Parfait is a delicious and creative way to use leftover desserts. Layer your favorite leftover desserts, such as cake, pudding, fruit, and whipped cream, in a glass or parfait dish.

You can also add a sprinkle of toppings like nuts, chocolate chips, or shaved coconut for extra flavor and texture, making it a perfect treat to share with the ones you love during the holiday season.

Yield: 4 Parfaits

Ingredients:

- 1 cup (250g/8.4 fl oz.) leftover cake, crumbled (assorted flavors work perfectly)

- 1 cup (250g/8.4 fl oz.) leftover pie, broken into small pieces
- ½ a cup (125g/4.05 fl oz.) leftover holiday cookies, crushed
- 1 cup (250ml/8.1 fl oz.) whipped cream
- ½ a cup (125ml/4.05 fl oz.) vanilla custard
- ¼ cup (60ml/2.02 fl oz.) cranberry sauce
- ¼ cup (60ml/2.02 fl oz.) chocolate sauce
- ¼ cup (60ml/2.02 fl oz.) chopped nuts (optional, for garnish)
- Fresh mint leaves (optional, for garnish)

Instructions:

1. Begin by gathering your leftover cake, pie, and cookies. Crumble the cake into small, bite-sized pieces, break the pastry into small chunks, and crush the cookies into fine crumbs. Set them aside.
2. In a separate dish, whip the cream until it reaches stiff peaks. If you prefer a drizzle of sweetness, add powdered sugar to the cream while beating.
3. In another bowl, combine the vanilla custard and cranberry sauce. Mix them until you achieve a beautiful, swirled effect.
4. Now it's time to assemble your parfait. Grab your serving glasses or bowls, and start with a layer of crumbled cake at the bottom. Use about a quarter of your cake.
5. Next, add a layer of broken pie pieces, followed by a layer of crushed cookies. The layers don't need to be perfectly even; aim for a harmonious blend of flavors and textures.
6. Spoon a dollop of the vanilla custard-cranberry sauce mixture on the cookie layer.
7. Continue layering with more cake, pie, and cookies, alternating with the custard-cranberry sauce mixture until you reach the top of your serving glasses.
8. Finish off with a generous dollop of whipped cream. Drizzle some chocolate sauce over the cream for that extra touch of indulgence.
9. If desired, garnish with chopped nuts and a sprig of fresh mint for a festive presentation.
10. Serve your Leftover Dessert Parfait immediately or refrigerate briefly to allow the flavors to meld.

Nutritional Information (Per Serving):

1 Parfait (Information May Differ Depending On Your Leftovers Used)

Calories: 350
Protein: 4g
Carbohydrates: 42g
Fat: 18g

Festive Pot Pie with All the Trimmings

This dish is a hearty, comforting meal perfect for special occasions or holiday gatherings.

The filling typically includes a variety of meats and vegetables, such as turkey, beef, or chicken, mixed with seasonings and spices. The crust is generally made with flour, butter, and eggs and can be topped with a crunchy pie crust or a flaky pastry.

To make the dish even more festive, you can add decorative toppings such as cherry tomatoes, making it a delightful centerpiece for your Christmas celebrations. Enjoy the enchanting flavors of the season as you indulge in this lovely holiday classic.

Yield: 1 Pot Pie (+-6 Servings)

Ingredients:

For the Filling:

- 2 cups (500g/16.06 fl oz.) cooked and diced turkey or chicken
- 1 cup (250g/8.4 fl oz.) cooked ham, cubed
- 1 cup (250g/8.4 fl oz.) cooked roast beef, cubed
- 2 cups (500g/16.06 fl oz.) mixed vegetables (carrots, peas, corn, and green beans)
- One small onion, finely chopped
- Three cloves garlic, minced
- ¼ cup (60g/2.02 fl oz.) unsalted butter
- ¼ cup (30g/1.05 oz.) plain flour
- 2 cups (500g/16.06 fl oz.) chicken or turkey broth
- 1 cup (250ml/8.4 fl oz.) whole milk
- One teaspoon(5g/0.16 oz.) of dried thyme
- Salt and black pepper, to taste

For the Crust:

- Two sheets of store-bought puff pastry thawed
- One egg, beaten (for egg wash)

Instructions:

1. Heat your oven up to 375°F (190°C).

2. In a sizable frying pan, melt the butter over medium heat. Add the chopped onions and minced garlic sauté until softened and aromatic.
3. Stir in the flour, creating a roux. Continue to cook for about 2 minutes, ensuring it's smooth and well combined.
4. Gradually pour in the chicken or turkey broth, followed by the whole milk, whisking continuously until the mixture thickens and becomes smooth—season with dried thyme, salt, and black pepper to your taste.
5. Add the cooked turkey or chicken, ham, roast beef, and mixed vegetables into the creamy sauce. Stir gently, ensuring all ingredients are well coated. Let it simmer for a few minutes until everything is heated through.
6. Transfer the savory filling into a deep pie dish, ensuring it's evenly distributed.
7. Unroll a single sheet of puff pastry and gently lay it over the filling, tucking in any excess pastry around the edges. Brush the top with an egg wash for a beautiful, golden finish.
8. Set the pie dish in the preheated oven and bake for 25-30 minutes or until the pastry is puffed and golden.
9. Once your Festive Pot Pie is out of the oven, rest for a few minutes before serving.

Nutritional Information (Per Serving):

1/6 or 1 Slice of The Pot Pie

Calories: 530
Protein: 37g
Carbohydrates: 37g
Fat: 25g

Chapter 8: Creating A Hygge Inspired Christmas

The crisp winter air outside is filled with the anticipation of Christmas, and inside, your home is adorned with cozy blankets, soft lighting, and the comforting scent of holiday spices. This is the essence of a Hygge-inspired Christmas, where warmth, togetherness, and simple pleasures take center stage. In this chapter, we will explore how to create a Hygge-inspired Christmas, blending the Danish concept of coziness with the magic of the holiday season.

Embrace the Simplicity of Hygge

At the heart of Hygge is the idea of simplicity and embracing the present moment. When celebrating Christmas with a Hygge touch, it's essential to simplify your decorations, meals, and activities. Choose natural and homemade elements to decorate your home, such as pine cones, evergreen branches, and candles. Opt for a real Christmas tree, and cut it down yourself. Choosing and decorating the tree together with loved ones can become a cherished tradition in itself.

The Art of Presenting

In the Hygge way, presentation is critical. Arrange your desserts with care, using natural and organic elements that complement the warmth of the holiday season. Wooden trays, rustic platters, and soft linen napkins create an inviting display. Add a touch of nature with sprigs of pine or holly, and remember to incorporate some of the candles that have been a staple throughout your Hygge-inspired Christmas.

Encourage your guests to serve themselves, passing around dessert plates and sharing the communal experience of indulging in sweet treats. The act of sharing and enjoying dessert together fosters a sense of togetherness and reinforces the Hygge spirit.

Creating a Hygge Feast

The key to a Hygge-inspired Christmas feast is simplicity, warmth, and togetherness. In a world that often rushes through the holiday season, we encourage you to take things slow, savor every moment, and embrace the Danish concept of "hygge" in your culinary traditions.

Traditional Comfort Foods

Start your Christmas feast with dishes that evoke a sense of nostalgia and warmth. Classic favorites like roast turkey or ham, mashed potatoes, and stuffing are always a hit. But don't be afraid to add your twist – perhaps a family recipe passed down through generations or a regional specialty that warms the hearts of your loved ones.

Hearty Soups and Stews

A pot of steaming, homemade soup, or stew is the perfect way to warm up your guests after a crisp winter's day. Consider comforting options like creamy tomato soup, hearty beef stew, or a nourishing chicken noodle soup. Serve it with freshly baked bread or rolls, allowing everyone to ladle their own portions, and encourage second helpings.

Sweet Delights

Desserts should be indulgent and heartwarming. Traditional favorites like apple pie, gingerbread cookies, and fruitcakes are always a hit. Consider involving your family in the baking process, making it a group activity that brings everyone together in the kitchen.

Cozy Beverages

Warm, inviting drinks are a cornerstone of Hygge celebrations. Offer a variety of beverages, from mulled wine and hot cider to rich hot chocolate. Make a station with a selection of toppings like whipped cream, cinnamon sticks, and marshmallows, allowing your guests to personalize their warm drinks.

Setting the Scene

Creating a Hygge atmosphere is not just about the food but also the surroundings and the experience. Set the scene for a memorable Christmas feast:

Cozy Table Setting

Dress your dining table in a way that encourages intimacy. Soft, warm colors, rustic tableware, and the gentle glow of candles on the table create a welcoming and Hygge-inspired atmosphere.

Candlelight and Ambiance

Candles play a significant role in the Hygge aesthetic. They create a warm and inviting space, which is perfect for a cozy Christmas celebration. Place candles throughout your home, especially on your dining table, where you'll enjoy your holiday feast. The soft glow of candlelight enhances the sense of togetherness and makes your space feel intimate and comforting.

Warm and Inviting Decor

For your Hygge-inspired Christmas, consider incorporating soft textures into your decor. Plush blankets, knitted pillows, and fluffy rugs will invite guests to curl up and get comfortable. These soft elements not only add warmth to your space but also create a sense of coziness that defines Hygge.

Decorating with natural and earthy tones, such as deep greens, rich reds, and warm browns, can also create a soothing ambiance that aligns with the Hygge philosophy. Adorn your home with tasteful, understated Christmas decorations.

Think natural elements like pinecones, evergreen branches, and soft twinkling lights. Incorporate handmade ornaments and create a warm and inviting ambiance without overwhelming the space.

Background Music

Enhance the atmosphere with a carefully curated playlist of soft, soothing Christmas tunes. The music should be in the background, setting the mood without overwhelming conversation and laughter.

Unplug and Connect

To fully embrace the Hygge philosophy during the holiday season, try to unplug from technology and connect with loved ones in person. Engage in old-fashioned activities like board games, storytelling, or simply sitting around the fire and talking. Put away the distractions and be fully present with the people who matter most.

Thoughtful Gestures

During your Christmas feast, consider incorporating some Danish traditions to deepen the Hygge experience. For instance, have a "Gækkebrev" exchange, where guests write anonymous notes filled with riddles and well-wishes for each other. The recipient must guess the sender and receive a small gift if they guess correctly.

Let the Conversation Flow

As your guests savor their desserts and hot beverages, engage in light-hearted conversations. Share stories and reminisce about past Christmases, or enjoy the moment's serenity. There's no rush to conclude the evening; instead, relish in the unhurried pleasure of one another's company.

Hygge is about savoring the small moments, including the post-feast conversations that allow you to connect with loved ones on a deeper level. Take the time to express your gratitude and appreciation for the shared warmth and coziness of the day.

Ending with Gratitude

As your Hygge-inspired Christmas feast comes to an end, remember to express your gratitude. Thank your guests for their presence and for sharing in the Hygge experience you've created. Acknowledge the effort that went into making this Christmas celebration memorable and recognize the simple yet meaningful joy that Hygge brings.

In the coming days, as you reflect on this Hygge Christmas feast, you'll find that it's not about extravagant gifts or elaborate decorations but the warmth of human connection and the beauty of simplicity that leaves a lasting impression.

Wrapping up a Hygge-inspired Christmas feast is about relishing the warmth of the holiday season and the contentment that can be found in the embrace of loved ones and the simple pleasures of life.

Homemade and Heartfelt

Christmas is an ideal time for DIY projects that bring a sense of satisfaction and personal touch to your celebrations. Consider making your ornaments, wreaths, and holiday crafts. Gather your family and friends to create these items, fostering a sense of togetherness and shared memories.

When it comes to gift-giving, choose presents that are thoughtful and heartfelt, as opposed to extravagant. A handmade gift or a handwritten note can carry immense meaning and Hygge spirit. Remember to accompany your dessert spread with a variety of warm beverages.

Hot chocolate with whipped cream, spiced chai tea, or a rich and aromatic coffee can be served with an array of toppings and flavorings to cater to everyone's taste. A delightful hot beverage can turn a simple dessert into an indulgent experience.

The Gift of Presence

Finally, the most precious gift you can give this Christmas is the gift of presence. Spend quality time with your loved ones, engaging in meaningful conversations and creating lasting memories. Whether through a winter hike, a carol-singing gathering, or simply sharing a quiet moment by the fire, the essence of a Hygge-inspired Christmas lies in the joy of togetherness.

Incorporating Hygge into your Christmas celebrations will help you slow down, appreciate the simple pleasures, and foster a sense of warmth and togetherness during this particular time of year. As you embrace the coziness and simplicity of the season, you'll discover that the true magic of Christmas lies in the heartfelt moments shared with loved ones.

Chapter 9: Creating Hygge Christmas Memories: Activities To Do Before A Meal

As the festive season approaches, the magic of Christmas takes center stage in our lives. The twinkling lights, the aroma of freshly baked cookies, and the warmth of loved ones coming together create a unique atmosphere of coziness and togetherness.

In this chapter, we will explore how to celebrate Christmas Hygge style by engaging in activities that will keep you and your loved ones entertained while creating precious memories that will last a lifetime.

Christmas Movie Marathon

Gather your family and friends, pop some corn, and snuggle up under a blanket to enjoy a Christmas movie marathon. Select a mix of your favorite classics and newer releases, and let the holiday spirit wash over you. Whether it's a heartwarming tale like "It's a Wonderful Life" or a humorous adventure like "Elf," there's a Christmas movie for everyone. Be sure to leave your worries at the door and immerse yourself in the heartwarming stories and festive cheer.

Christmas Baking Extravaganza

Baking is a beloved holiday tradition, and there's no better time to indulge in it than during the Christmas season. Gather your loved ones and spend a cozy day in the kitchen, creating a variety of sweet treats like gingerbread cookies, fruitcakes, or peppermint brownies. The process of baking together not only warms the house with delicious scents but also provides a perfect opportunity for bonding.

Handmade Christmas Decorations

Get creative and make your own Christmas decorations. Whether crafting paper snowflakes, stringing popcorn garlands, or creating personalized ornaments, crafting together fosters a sense of togetherness and ensures that your Christmas décor is imbued with love and personal touches.

Caroling and Sing-Alongs

Bring out your inner caroller by singing your favorite Christmas carols with your loved ones. If you're feeling more adventurous, you can even organize a neighborhood caroling event to spread cheer to your neighbors. Music has the incredible power to bond people and create a warm, Hygge atmosphere.

Winter Nature Walks

If you live in an area where snow falls during the holiday season, take advantage of it by going for a winter nature walk. Bundle up in warm clothing and explore the wintry landscape with your loved ones. The serene beauty of a snow-covered forest or park is an excellent backdrop for meaningful conversations and bonding.

Gift Wrapping Party

Turn the chore of gift wrapping into a joyful occasion by making it a group effort. Gather your friends or family, put on some festive music, and make a game out of it. Compare creative gift-wrapping ideas and enjoy the satisfaction of perfectly wrapped presents.

Reading Stories by the Fireplace

There's nothing quite like the soft glow of a crackling fire to create a cozy, Hygge atmosphere. Gather your loved ones around the fireplace, sip hot cocoa or mulled wine, and take turns reading classic Christmas stories or sharing your favorite holiday memories.

Secret Santa Gift Exchange

Instead of focusing on expensive gifts, organize a Secret Santa gift exchange with family and friends. Set a budget, draw names, and give thoughtful, personalized gifts that show you know each other well. The element of surprise and the joy of giving and receiving heartfelt gifts make this activity truly Hygge.

Volunteer Together

Spread the spirit of Christmas by volunteering as a group. Whether at a local food bank, a shelter, or a charitable organization, helping those in need during the holiday season is an enriching way to bond with loved ones and create everlasting memories.

Hygge-Inspired Gift Making

Spend time crafting personalized gifts for your loved ones. Whether it's knitting cozy scarves, creating scented candles, or designing custom photo albums, the act of making something by hand adds a special touch to your holiday celebrations. It's a beautiful way to show appreciation and love for those who matter most.

Hygge Games Night

Gather around the table for a cozy games night featuring your favorite board games or card games. Whether you're a fan of competitive board games or prefer a laid-back card game, the laughter and friendly competition will warm your hearts and create memories you'll look back on with a smile.

Holiday Light Tour

Embark on a magical journey to explore the best Christmas light displays in your town or city. Load up the car with hot cocoa and cozy blankets, and drive through neighborhoods renowned for their festive decorations. Admire the creativity of your fellow community members, and let the twinkling lights infuse your evening with Hygge magic.

Reflect and Set Intentions for the New Year

Take a moment to pause and reflect on the year that has passed. Share your highlights and lessons with your loved ones, then set intentions for the upcoming year. Whether discussing personal goals and resolutions or simply expressing gratitude for the present, this activity will foster a greater sense of connection and shared purpose.

Hygge and Yoga

Bring mindfulness into your holiday season with a family or friends yoga session. Roll out your yoga mats in a cozy, well-lit space, and follow along with a guided yoga practice designed for all skill levels.

Encourage each other to find balance and serenity amidst the holiday hustle and bustle.

Letter to Your Future Self

Take a seat with your loved ones and write letters to your future selves, sharing your hopes and dreams for the next Christmas season. Seal the letters in envelopes and promise to open them together next year. It's a beautiful way to connect with your loved ones and witness your personal growth over time.

Midnight Mass or Candlelight Service

For those who celebrate Christmas within a religious context, attending a midnight mass or candlelight service can be a profoundly moving and Hygge experience. The soft candlelight, uplifting hymns, and the sense of community in these sacred moments can provide a serene and spiritual aspect to your holiday celebrations.

Hygge Gift Exchange Ceremony

Incorporate the Danish concept of "Hyggekrog" into your gift-giving tradition. Designate a comfortable and cozy corner of your home as the "Hyggekrog," where gifts are exchanged. Light candles, arrange plush cushions and create an intimate setting. Each person takes turns presenting their gifts with a personal touch, sharing the story or sentiment behind their chosen presents. This added layer of thoughtfulness will make your gift exchange a truly Hygge experience.

Christmas Morning Breakfast Feast

Start Christmas Day on a cozy note by preparing a delicious breakfast spread. Serve freshly baked pastries, warm cinnamon rolls, and other delightful treats. Encourage everyone to come to the table in their pajamas and relish the first moments of Christmas together, savoring good food and even better company.

Hygge-Style Outdoor Activities

Embrace the serene beauty of the winter season with outdoor activities that promote Hygge. Go ice skating at a local rink, build a snowman, or take a peaceful nature hike. Spending time outdoors and fostering a connection with nature can bring peace and contentment to your holiday celebrations.

Hygge-Themed Potluck Dinner

Host a Hygge-inspired potluck dinner with friends and family. Encourage everyone to bring a comforting dish and representative of their personal Hygge experience. Sharing a diverse range of cozy dishes and recipes can be a delightful culinary adventure fostering a sense of community.

Hygge Affirmation Cards

Create a set of Hygge affirmation cards with words of comfort, encouragement, and gratitude. Take turns drawing cards and sharing the affirmations. This activity can bring a sense of mindfulness to your holiday celebrations and remind you of the simple joys in life.

Hygge Home Decorating Contest

Turn decorating your home into a friendly competition. Challenge your family and friends to create the coziest and most inviting Hygge-inspired spaces. Participants can bring their unique touch to the decorations and then come together to admire and vote on the winner. It's a fun and creative way to bond and celebrate the Hygge spirit.

Hygge Storytelling Circle

Gather in a circle, either indoors around a warm fire or outdoors beneath the starry winter sky. Share stories from your past Christmases, fond memories, and heartwarming tales that have shaped your holiday traditions. As each person takes a turn, not only do you strengthen your connection with loved ones, but you also gain a deeper appreciation for the shared history that has brought you to this moment.

Hygge-Themed Charity Auction

Combine the spirit of giving with an element of fun by organizing a Hygge-themed charity auction. Each participant brings an item or service to auction off, and the proceeds are donated to a charitable cause. This heartwarming activity reinforces the idea of spreading warmth and goodwill during the Christmas season.

Hygge Family Photo Session

Capture the essence of Hygge by scheduling a family photo session. Whether it's a professional photographer or a DIY session with a tripod and timer, the goal is to capture candid moments of togetherness, warmth, and love. These photos will become cherished memories for years, reminding you of the Hygge atmosphere you created during the holiday season.

Hygge Hot Chocolate Bar

Set up a Hygge-inspired hot chocolate bar with an array of toppings like whipped cream, marshmallows, chocolate shavings, and flavored syrups. Invite your loved ones to personalize their warm mugs of hot chocolate. As you sip this comforting beverage, engage in meaningful conversations and relish the simple pleasures of life.

Hygge-Inspired Gift of Time

Incorporate the Danish concept of "hyggegave," which involves giving the gift of time or experiences rather than material presents. Create a "hyggegave" calendar for the upcoming year, including plans for cozy movie nights, nature hikes, homemade dinners, or even spa days. Exchange these thoughtful experiences with your loved ones and prioritize spending time together in the coming months.

Hygge Family Scrapbooking

Gather around the table with a plethora of old photographs, mementos, and crafting supplies. Spend an afternoon or evening creating a family scrapbook highlighting your fondest memories. As you reminisce and create together, you'll be reminded of the value of shared experiences and the importance of preserving them.

Hygge-Inspired Gratitude Jar

Set up a "gratitude jar" in your home throughout the Christmas season. Encourage everyone to jot down moments of gratitude, kindness, or joy on small slips of paper and place them in the jar. On Christmas Day or New Year's Eve, read the notes aloud as a reminder of the many reasons to be grateful and to celebrate the Hygge spirit of appreciation.

Incorporating these activities into your holiday season will help you create a Hygge Christmas full of warmth, togetherness, and cherished memories. Remember, it's not about the grand gestures but the small moments of connection and love that truly make the holiday season unique. So, embrace the Hygge spirit and celebrate Christmas in a way that fills your heart with joy and gratitude.

Conclusion

Amid the festive season, there's something genuinely magical about gathering with loved ones, sharing laughter, and savoring delicious dishes that warm the heart and the soul. These 35 hyggelig Christmas recipes have not only provided us with a culinary journey but have also woven a sense of togetherness and coziness into the very fabric of the holiday season.

As we explored these recipes, we discovered the joy of crafting homemade treats that fill our homes with enticing aromas and our hearts with pure delight. From the comfort of a crackling fireplace to the twinkle of holiday lights, these dishes have been a reminder that the true essence of Christmas lies not only in the grand gestures but also in the simple, intimate moments shared around the dinner table.

From the rich, velvety hot chocolate that warms us on a chilly winter's night to the delightful gingerbread cookies that adorn our homes with sweet nostalgia, these recipes have allowed us to create cherished traditions and build lasting memories. They have rekindled the appreciation for the art of slow cooking, the satisfaction of kneading dough by hand, and the wonder of creating edible masterpieces.

In a world filled with hustle and bustle, these hyggelig Christmas recipes beckon us to slow down and savor the season. They encourage us to revel in the act of giving, not just receiving, and to treasure the time spent in the company of those we hold dear. It's a reminder that the warmth of the season comes not only from the fireplace but from the connections we nurture and the love we share.

So, as we embark on this festive season with our aprons on and our hearts open, let these 35 hyggelig Christmas recipes serve as a guide to not just preparing food but creating moments of joy, love, and togetherness. May they help us find solace in the simple pleasures of life, and may our kitchens become a sanctuary of happiness and celebration, echoing with laughter and the clinking of glasses. Ultimately, it's not just about the food; it's about the love and hygge spirit we infuse into each bite, making the festive season truly special and memorable.

Made in United States
Orlando, FL
24 November 2024

54362451R00065